ለአባታችንና ለንጉሡ ነገሥታችን ለቀዳማዊ
ኃይለ ሥላሴ ዘመነ መንግሥት፥
በመድኃኒታችን በኢየሱስ ክርስቶስ በጌቶች
ጌታችን ክቡር ስም ታላቅ ምስጋናችንን
እናቀርባለን።

We present our many thanks to Our God-Father and to Our King of Kings, to His Imperial Majesty, HAILE SELLASSIE I's Kingdome in the Glorious name of *Iyesus Kristos*, Our Saviour – Our Lord of Lords.

AMEN AND AMEN.

The Bible Society Of
His Imperial Majesty (BSHIM)

Published By: H.H. Ras Iadonis Tafari,
& H.H. Woizero Tehetena Girma-Asfaw
of The Lion of Judah Society (LOJS)

Imperial Publishers to the H.I.M. Universities, Colleges & Christian [Tewahedo] Churches

©1991-2011 Bshim-Loj

©2011 by LION OF JUDAH SOCIETY PUBLISHERS & IYOBELYU [JUBILEE] PRINTING PRESS

ISBN: 1500631132

All rights reserved. No part of this publication may be reproduced or transmitted for commercial purposes, except for brief quotations in printed reviews, without written permission of the publishers'.

Churches and other noncommercial interests may reproduce portions of this book without the express written permission of the LOJS PUBLISHERS, provided that the text does not exceed 500 words and that the text is not material quoted from another publisher. When reproducing text from this book, include the following credit line: "From *Rastafari Preliminary Notes on the H.I.M. Haile Selassie I [Amharic] Bible: An Introduction to the Book of the Seven Seals,* published by the Lion of Judah Society. Used by permission."

All English-language scripture quotations, unless otherwise noted, are taken from the King James Version of the 1611 A.D. Holy Bible [KJV].

All Amharic-language scripture quotations, unless otherwise noted, are taken the *Emperor's Bible,* the 1961/2 A.D. Authorized H.I.M. HAILE SELLASSIE I Revised Amharic Bible [RAB].

Published by THE LION OF JUDAH SOCIETY, www.lojsociety.org

Our mission is to bring good tidings, that publisheth peace; that bringeth good tidings of good, that saith to Zion, Thy God reigneth. – Isaiah 52:7

Printed in the United States of America.

RasTafari
Preliminary Notes

on the

H.I.M. Haile Selassie I
Amharic Bible:
An Introduction to the Book of Seven Seals
The 1954 A.M. [1961 A.D.] *"Emperor's Bible,"*
By: Ras Iadonis Tafari
First Edition

Published in the 400th Anniversary Year of the first printing and publication of the King James Version of the 1611 A.D. Holy Bible.

This edition has also been published in the 50th Anniversary, or Jubilee Year of the very first printing and publication of the Emperor's Revised Amharic Bible, the Imperial Authorized Version of the Ethiopian Holy Bible, published originally on the 23rd of July 1961 A.D.

የዮሐንስ ወንጌል 1፥14

ቃልም ሥጋ ሆነ፤ ጸጋንና እውነትንም ተመልቶ በእኛ አደረ፤ አንድ ልጅም ከአባቱ ዘንድ እንዳለው ክብር የሆነው ክብሩን አየን።

እኔ አባት እሆነዋለሁ እርሱም ልጅ ይሆነኛል
— ወደ ዕብራውያን 1:5

መጽሐፍ ቅዱስ
The "Seven Seals" (Sebatun Makhtem) of the "Book"

Pictured above is the actual prophetic *"seven seals"* (sebatun makhtem) found on the "backside" or 'spine' of the "book of the seven seals" as revealed to the lost-found sheep, i.e. the anointed Ethiopian-Hebrews and elect Rastafari of the western diaspora of the biblical "ISRAEL" by the "Repairer of the breach, the Restorer of the way to tabernacle/dwell," (Isaiah 58:12), our Aframerican brother, disciple and fellow co-labourer: Ras Iadonis Tafari in 1991 AD after the *"half an hour space in heaven"* (Revelations 8:1).

« [ነገር ግን] አሳቤን በመንፈሴ ኃይል ሁሉ ከልቤ ለመናገር የሚቻለኝ በአማርኛ ቋንቋ ስለ ሆነ ፩ »

"[*But as it is*] **In the Amharic language alone** that I am able to speak my mind from my heart and with all the force of my spirit;"

My Life and Ethiopia's Progress: The Autobiography of Emperor Haile Sellassie I; taken from page 299; pg. 253 in the Amharic Version –

ቀዳማዊ ኃይለ ሥላሴ ንጉሠ ነገሥት
ሕይወቴና የኢትዮጵያ እርምጃ.

Newsday / Ned Levine

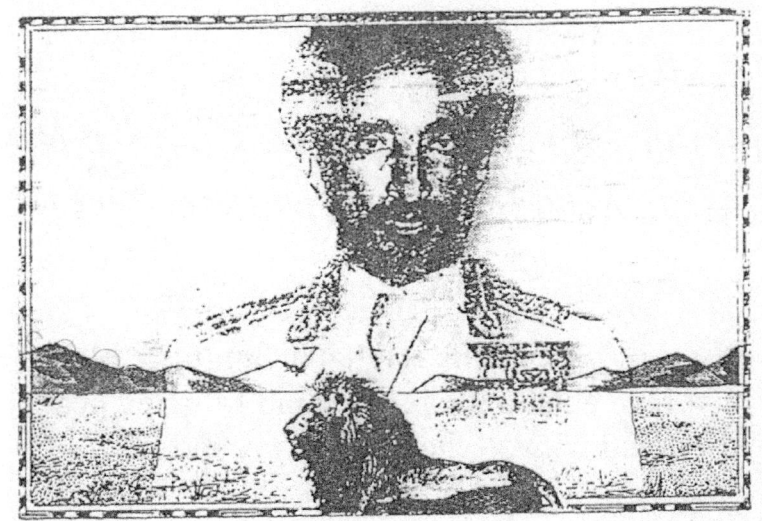

PREFATORY NOTES

TO THE H.I.M. HAILE SELASSIE REVISED 1961 AD AMHARIC BIBLE,

ALSO KNOWN AS,

"THE BOOK OF THE SEVEN SEALS" REVELATION CHAPTER 5, VERSE 5

My primary reason and main intent for composing this edition of the book, and this initial attempt to respond to the interest and accompanying questions and inquiries addressed concerning the H.I.M. HAILE SELASSIE 1961 AUTHORIZED REVISED [AMHARIC] BIBLE, the Bible in Amharic and the heartfelt desire to share the Word of the Living God with both "Jew and Gentile" Whether it is a good translation, we have no doubt, especially when this is considered based upon the most ancient Hebrew and Greeks language texts and other Ethiopic MSS currently available to us. In brief detail, some of these will be dealt with, at a basic introductory level by reference to pre-existing scholarship of the subject in the Western tradition in general.

However, I did not expect to have to write a brief biography – yet, this seems to me now to be necessary, although not a prerequisite, to this discussion of the Amharic Bible or related transaction. I will summarize as follows: Namely, I – the present author, believe – and better still, have the living faith and active knowledge in the GOD AND FATHER OF OUR LORD AND SAVIOUR JESUS CHRIST. The Holy Bible, as I am now more thoroughly persuaded and spiritually convinced, is the main guide – along with the Holy Spirit – for any and all those who are inclined to acknowledge the same, and like myself, do not subscribe much credence to the hosts of modern schools of religious scribes and Pharisees, or even Sadducees – whether of the catholic or of the Eastern orthodoxy brands that have co-created what we now know as the abominations of the Ecclesiastical hierarchies that have defectively divided the Christian brotherhood – the fraternity of the Christ between themselves into the so-called clergy and the laity. Study of the bible proves how this error in Gentile, or the *"Romantic,"* mistranslations that occurred ages ago, beginning around the time of Ignatius, whom we do not regard as a "Saint" – sadly, those who do have also, knowingly or in such ignorance – effectively prevented access to the "laity" over the ages even to the point of much innocent bloodshed and the abomination known as the "inquisition."

The very Word of God – the λογοσ , as contained in the Holy Bible, irrespective of translation or preferred version – is the starting point to righting these some of these wrongs of the earlier and even present forms, versions and perversions of so-called Christianity that we are confronted with today. As His Imperial Majesty, HAILE SELASSIE I, has so clearly stated and said:

"WE IN ETHIOPIA HAVE ONE OF THE OLDEST VERSIONS OF THE BIBLE, but however old the version may be, in whatever language it might be written, the Word[1] remains one and the same. It transcends all boundaries of empires and all conceptions of race. It is eternal.[2]"

As for myself, the present author, I was born into an African-American, or Aframerican[3] Christian[4]-based home, and there became thoroughly introduced to the *Antiquities of the Black Race*[5] — a still yet to be "officially" published manuscript

---

[1] It must be noted that when His Majesty mentions and refers to "the word" here, the Emperor is not speaking of the mere words or translations of men, rather the Word in the person of the λογοσ Logos, i.e. Jesus Christ incarnate.

[2] "We in Ethiopia" Speech is undated and often referred to as the H.I.M. Haile Selassie I on the Bible Speech by H.I.M. Haile Selassie I, translated by Haile Selassie I Press.

[3] Was the term used by Black Americans, especially the writers, poets and intellectuals in the United States around the turn of the 20th century; especially in the 1920s and 30s. Most of the early documents on Ethiopia, especially those by J.A. Rodgers – author of *The Truth About Ethiopia*, and other Ethiopianist authors used this term extensively. Sadly, it has come into disuse amongst the present generation.

[4] My Christian upbringing is largely credited to two important women, or 'Mothers," – namely, my 'Nana' or "grandmother" whose name was Sarah-Ann Wilson and her adopted daughter, my maternal mother, Sarah Louise.

[5] A four-part series of essays on the ancient history, the antiquity and biblical origins of the black race composed by my father to rebut the prevailing racism in White Western scholasticism.

by my late and beloved earthly father[6], that was partially disseminated [part one of four] in the Nation of Islam's newspaper in the early 1970s. This detailed research paper inspired my own subsequent investigations into, and diligently study of, the history of the bible, the origins of early Christianity and, of course – the ancient and blameless Ethiopians – *the Wonderful Ethiopians of the Kushite Empire*[7]. Through my father's encouragement, and his oft made and very passionate references to these ancient Abyssinians or Kamites, whom he accurately identified as 'our people,' namely – the biblical "HAMITES" and "CUSHITES" I began my own education into Abyssinia, or should I say, biblical Æthiopia and the testimony of His Imperial Majesty, HAILE SELASSIE I and his attempts to reform the theological errors and religious compromises that crept into the [Ethiopian] Orthodoxy of the ancient 4th century Church of Ethiopia, pseudonymously referred to as "ABYSSINIAN Church." The Emperor's own openness to Western missionaries and African-Americans interested in Ethiopian Christianity attracted me to learn more about His Imperial

---

[6] My step-father's Arabic and Islamic name was Rafiyq Ahmed Abdul-Hamiyd and his [White; or, Anglo-American] Christian name was Ralph Raymond Gaillard. He was an Arabic teacher and had started the AL-HAMIYDIYYAH ACADEMY OF ARABIC in my childhood. I was introduced to Arabic, or *Arabiyya Fusha* – or Qur'anic Arabic and Semitic studies. Arabic, therefore was my first language and I credit him highly for his influence linguistically and academically.

[7] An excellent book written by Drusilla Dunjee Houston; a must read!

Majesty [abbreviated as H.I.M.], His divine lineage and the works of His faith that have been both ignored and when mentioned, misrepresented and slandered in this present world. It is a perfect example of the parable, nay I say the ancient *mythos* that speaks of the refusal to and rejection of the "Stone" who becomes the "Head cornerstone," – the Head of the corner, being disallowed by the proverbial 'builders' in the Psalm of David [Psalms 118, Verse 22]. But this, as intended, will be taken up in suitable details later on other appropriate volumes of present writing devoted to the said subjects.

PSALMS OF DAVID 118, VERSE 22

ግንበኞች የናቁት ድንጋይ፥ እርሱ የማዕዘን ራስ ሆነ፥

"The stone which the builders refused is become the head *stone* of the corner."

Therefore, when I say respectively – that my own "calling" in Christ, the Anointed Messiah has led me, step by step as a member of Ethiopic branch of Ancient Christianity [Tewahedo]. True Christianity is *Rastafari*, and this *Rastafari* "calling" is not to a sect or an –ism, however – it is based upon and must be considered in the light of H.I.M. HAILE SELASSIE I'S own clear, concise and bible-based testimony of JESUS CHRIST. Without such light and illumination we would continue to walk on stumbling blindly in darkness of error and ignorance. [St. John Chapter 1, Verse 5] His [Amharic] Bible, therefore, likened to the "[Book of the] Tree of Life" produces the fruits of the spirit, His unfeigned labours of His love to usward working by faith. Many cannot comprehend the "light," nor apprehend it apart from a true birth, that is the New Birth. "Verily, verily, I say to thee, Except a man be born again, he cannot enter the kingdom of God." [St. John Chapter 3, Verse 3] This re-birth is called regeneration and there is a vital prerequisite need and necessity for us to be born again and to follow the "Son of Man" in the regeneration.

St. Matthew Chapter 19, Verses 28-29

ኢየሱስም እንዲህ አላቸው፦ እውነት እላችኋለሁ፤ እናንተስ የተከተላችሁኝ፤ በዳግመኛ ልደት የሰው ልጅ በክብሩ ዙፋን በሚቀመጥበት ጊዜ፤ እናንተ ደግሞ በአሥራ ሁለቱ የእስራኤል ነገድ ስትፈርዱ በአሥራ ሁለት ዙፋን ትቀመጣላችሁ። ስለ ስሜም ቤቶችን ወይም ወንድሞችን ወይም እኅቶችን ወይም አባትን ወይም እናትን ወይም ሚስትን ወይም ልጆችን ወይም እርሻን የተወ ሁሉ መቶ እጥፍ ይቀበላል የዘላለምንም ሕይወት ይወርሳል። "Verily I say to you, that ye who have followed me, in the regeneration [or, *Re-Birth*] when the Son of man shall sit on the throne of his glory, ye also shall sit upon twelve thrones, judging the twelve tribes of Israel. And every one that hath left houses, or brethren, or sisters, or father, or mother, or children, or lands, for my name's sake, shall receive a hundredfold, and shall inherit eternal life."

The true faith, TEWAH'DO HAYMANOT, should not be confused with *the many* who may say "Lord, Lord[8]," claiming to come in His name, but knowingly, or by default of ignorance – deny His clear and obvious testimony of the True faith.

Based upon all this, and so much more, I myself affirm the call and acknowledge the chosen responsibility to minister "CHRIST IN HIS KINGLY CHARACTER" in His New Name [Revelation Chapter 3, Verse 12; 2:17; 19:12 compare with St. John 1:42], to preach the "Message of Salvation." This Ethiopic *reformation*, amongst both the Ethiopian Christians and many of my beloved RASTAFARI brethren, is squarely based upon the True Gospel of the last True Emperor of Ethiopia, H.I.M. HAILE SELLASSIE I, encouraging them all in and through the Good News – to all that will listen and take heed to the King of kings' testimony[9]. We must not to get too overwhelmed by the lure of the pomp, pride and ceremony so often associated and found in outer forms of

---

[8] Matthew 7:21-22; Luke 6:46

[9] The best evidence known to this author of the said "King of kings testimony," is to be found in the Selected Speeches and Public Utterances of the Emperor, especially the Lutheran Interview or better known as the Haile Selassie Christmas Interview with Dr. Oswald Hoffman – dated December 25th 1968. A full translated copy of the Interview is to be included at the appendix to this volume.

Ethiopian so-called Orthodoxy[10] or "Egyptian [Orthodox] Domination[11]," rather than that, it is good and useful indeed to return to the simple roots of the faith and example expounded by His Majesty in Jesus Christ and to continue to grow in His word, the Holy Bible.

Over the nearly 19 years since I first became acquainted with His Majesty's [Amharic] Bible, I have become better qualified to discuss and willing to share the insights I also have gained regarding the accuracy of H.I.M. Haile Selassie I's 1960/61 AD Revised [Amharic] Bible translation vis-à-vis, say – the King James Version [KJV] of the Bible known and celebrated in the West as an authority. The Hebrew and Greek scrolls and manuscripts that underlie the KJV have also been reviewed, discussed and diligently compared with the Ethiopic MSS which are, in fact, older, more accurate and

---

[10] A better definition must be given on the distinction and difference between indigenous Orthodox pre-4th century and post. This will explain His Majesty's intent and urgency in establishing autonomy or the status of autocephaly for the Ethiopian [Tewahedo] Orthodox Church after the lapse of 1600 years.

[11] Here we must mention the last appointed Nibura-Id, or "Keeper of the Holy City of Aksum [Axum]," named Ermias Kebede Wolde-Yesus who has brought to light many important facts, previously suppressed, concerning the Egyptian Orthodox church's [religious] influence and domination of the indigeous Ethiopic Tewahedo, or "Orthodox" church, pre-4th century. A further exploration of this matter is proposed and intended by the present Author, who has been encouraged by recent conversations with the Nibura-Id via the his online publication concerning the indigenous Orthodoxy and the foreign [Egyptian] domination inclusive of the prophetic role and fulfillment of the faithful Rastafarian movement and this present "mixed multitude"generation of Ethiopians, at home and abroad.

originally the basis of the *Masoretic* reforms of the Age of Ezra and Nehemiah. We hope that we have studied to show ourselves approved, if only to share with those willing to learn what we have ourselves learned over the many years.

H.H. RAS IADONIS TAFARI

305A Halsey Street
Brooklyn, New York
December, 2010

Introduction

DEAR READER – take note that – any book or document so written about His Imperial Majesty's Holy [Amharic] Bible, especially, must include axiomatically, as a matter of fact, some testimony of the movement that bears and is inspired by His Holy Name, i.e. RASTAFARI and the Rastafarians. In the previous draft and summary compositions to this present volume, the present writer had originally conceived to compose a brief and summary composition that would focus more exclusively on the Rastafarian movement's relationship with its namesake and the rightful role of the HAILE SELASSIE I REVISED AMHARIC BIBLE 1961/62 MSS.

However, it was duly observed, in the process of these preliminary drafts, that additional attention in *this* present work should be given to a brief synopsis, as it may be, of some of the main and previously published Ethiopic MSS and Amharic bible translations – and the rare and scant scholarship – prior to, and ultimately culminating in the Revised Amharic Bible published by His Imperial Majesty's BERHANNINA SELAM Printing Press in 1961 AD. The majority of serious research and scholarly studies have concerned itself with Ethiopic and the Bible. The documents devoted to the "Amharic," in light of the Bible and the Hebrew Bible, or Torah are rarer still besides the attempts of the Missionaries who have generally been consigned to literally retranslate their own English texts into some form of vernacular Amharic or other Ethiopian dialect. Yet, that is not of primary concern to us as those versions only highlight the external influences of the Gentiles in disseminating the Gospel based upon their Western revisions, and numerous versions; and must not be confused or confounded with the indigenous growth and progress of the native [ETHIOPIC] Holy Bible. Thus, any documentation of this kind is quite rare and very hard-to-find; with a few noteworthy exceptions that we will like to note, as cursory as possible and in a few words designed as a general reference for the students interested in their own further studies and research upon the matter.

Firstly, there was Hiob Ludolph, also spelt Job Ludolf from Gotha who contributed much and many of the earliest MSS documents such as the Ethiopic Psalms and a host of lexicons written in Latin and handwritten Ethiopic [Ge'ez]. Most were liturgical and comparative between the Romanist and the "Abyssinian" church orders. His works have been filed under Latin and Aethiopica manuscripts, most dated as early as 1630s. Ludolf was basically following up on the work begun by the Romanists and Catholic Missionaries, the Jesuits in Ethiopia since the mid-1500s. However, their mission was to bring the Ethiopian Christians under the "Authority of the Pope." Thus, their documents betray these attempts to probe for strengths and weaknesses; similarities and differences and so forth. This is a subject that deserves special treatment.

But, for us and our purposes here it was the Reverend Carl William Isenberg who wrote a two part volume, an Amharic Dictionary and an Amharic Grammar book based upon Biblical references in details, especially on the old dialectical Amharic language, leading to the classical forms of the nineteenth century. We would like to make mention with honours of Rev. C.W. Isenberg's work, mainly from a missionary perspective – it is extremely noteworthy, especially in his Amharic Dictionary, one of the first of its kind in the attention and detailed references to Hebraic and Biblical correlations between the Hebrew, Ethiopic and archaic Amharic that reminds us of the scholarship of August Dillmann, the great German linguist whose work, Ethiopic Grammar, is still relevant and has not been surpassed in kind to this day. The focal point of Isenberg's work was mainly the Amharic language, while Dillmann was preeminently involved with several major ETHIOPIC or GE'EZ transactions, namely manuscript translations and early Ethiopic Orthodox church documents – most were known of but had never before been read outside of Ethiopia or the Ethiopian languages, from Apocryphal MSS like the BOOK OF ENOCH [DAS

BUCH HENOCH] to Little Genesis, otherwise known as the BOOK OF JUBILEES [LIBER JUBILAEORUM], to name a few. This is not to compare the respective works of two of our favorite *éthiopisants*, Isenberg and Dillmann, rather it is to distinguish their recommended works and specialties, or Academic strengths, one from another for the present purposes being noted here for the reader, who may be somewhat unfamiliar with the history of Ethiopic studies in the Western, and particularly, the European scholarship.

Revd. Isenberg, like many of his predecessors and contemporaries, being a Christian missionary, had such a scripture-based approach towards the Abyssinian, or Ethiopian highland peoples via the Amharic language based upon his intention to further disseminate the Gospels of Our Lord and Saviour. Professor Dillmann, on the other hand, also being a man of God, and an accomplished linguist and scholar, was more interested, it would appear based upon the evidence, in the ancient Ethiopic-Hebrew or Semitic roots, both culturally and linguistically of the Ethiopic [Orthodox] Church as contained and preserved in the literature and rare manuscripts of these relatively isolated highland peoples of the horn of Africa's *biblical* regions. These two noteworthy scholars, it must be said here, were also separated by a least a generation and therefore were not in any way competitors but rather enabled to compliment each others outstanding scholarship bequeathing a virtual wealth of ancient knowledge to those of us have been blest in the diligent perusing, oft reading and detailed study of their respective efforts, historical documentation and variety of manuscripts still accessible to us today.

Credit is thus duly owed to them, amongst many others, before and after their time – their names and accolades too numerous to list here, yet they, for their part, kept the Ethiopic and Amharic Bible studies academically relevant during an age of *Eurocentricism* when Abyssinia, or "Ethiopia" was not to be taken very serious by the majority of the Romanists, European and Anglo-American "bibliolators" – an appropriate term coined by Mr. Gerald Massey to identify the 'supreme delusion of the European mind, and the crowning error of all time.' [See Gerald Massey's Lectures, pg 249]

The majority of the so-called Anglo-Hebraists – like most of the Victorian school of Egyptologists – Sir Ernest Alfred Wallis Thompson Budge here included, vainly and extremely concededly thought that most or even all of the ancient Ethiopic MSS were merely slavish translations or copies from either the prevailing Septuagint Greek or even the Masoretic, squared *Chaldean*, Hebrew versions of the Bible which are considerably later in date than the oldest Ethiopic [GE'EZ]. Dillmann attempted to prove this in his excellent work entitled, "ETHIOPIC GRAMMAR" where he showed and provided tangible etymological and linguistic proof of Ethiopic's embedded Hebraic elements, overlooked by most others who had access to the same source material MSS.

Ethiopic and now Amharic scholarship since, thanks be to the Almighty, has matured enough to finally recognize and accept the fact that the many of the oldest biblical manuscripts, namely, the Old Testament MSS documents, faithfully preserved in the Ethiopic are indeed considerably older than the so-called Masoretic *textus receptus* and, moreover, in many details, even the New Testament Ethiopic MSS is also more accurate than the SEPTUAGINT or LXX. As a testimony to this fact, we have one Hailu Habtu, an Ethiopian scholar and author of "Preliminary Notes in Ethiopian Studies" [published by the City College of New York – c. 1992]. This document has indeed shed much needed light and illumination on such matters alluded to above, namely those concerning the antiquity and accuracy of the Ethiopic Old and New Testament MSS in his preliminary notes that demand a fuller hearing and exposition of. Suffice it to say, this too will have to be addressed in another volume devoted more exclusively to the subject matter of the received Ethiopic MSS, during the time of Ezra and Nehemiah – producing, according to the Mr. Hailu's references, the current recession known as MASORETIC MSS and the present Hebrew Bible, the Jewish TANAKH or modern Judaism's received Torah scrolls – an important dissertation, no doubt, one of several proposed, that is entirely beyond the scope of the present work and hopefully will be followed up in another volume devoted exclusively to its fuller exposition.

However, one of the few documents, known to this author, that has seriously attempted to address the ልሳነ፡ነገሥ *lesane Negus*, i.e. biblical Amharic language and the very matter at hand, that is, of the Amharic Bible and its translations, in our humble opinion, is the rare volume written by the imminent scholar and researcher, Edward Ullendorff entitled "Ethiopia and The Bible" – The Schweich Lectures published for the British Academy by the Oxford University Press in 1967 AD. In Chapter 1 of Mr. Ullendorff's volume entitled appropriately "BIBLE TRANSLATIONS" is a noteworthy preliminary document and series of essays that enables us, at the present, to undertake a more critical view of the said subject at this time. We must here again give due thanks to Mr. Ullendorff for his many contributions, translations [including the Autobiography of His Imperial Majesty, My Life and Ethiopia's

Progress, Vol. 1] and other transactions related to Ethiopia, His Majesty and the corpus of literature generally termed "ETHIOPIC STUDIES."

However, much like Mr. Ullendorff, we must also make the claim here that even our present composition must also be considered in and of itself only 'a survey rather than a study in depth.'

The German scholar, August Dillmann, who we have already named and praised in regard to the study of Ethiopic language and its body of literature, was unable to complete all that he intended or set out to, largely due to his sudden death. Not only that, but his apprentice's untimely death as well, both very suspicious, caused the future of Ethiopic study of the time to be suspended indefinitely until the very recent times. A rather well researched volume called ETHIOPIC, AN AFRICAN WRITING SYSTEM; ITS HISTORY AND PRINCIPLES by a native Ethiopian writer named AYELE BEKERIE is one such work that has renewed some interest in Ethiopic and Ethiopian linguistic studies. However, sadly, the Amharic Bible of His Majesty has not be given any critical, detailed study or even its due consideration; overwhelmingly ignored by many or most of the predominant past and present scholars and researchers in the field of Biblical and Eastern Language scholarship.

The reasons or rather – the excuses – for such Eurocentric scholastic apathy, obfuscation and overtly blatant racism and racial bias to Ethiopia and Her Blameless Emperor are too numerous and varied to be discuss here at the present time. Besides, they do not concern us as they have been proven without merit and erroneous. Their names have been forgotten and their efforts to deny Ethiopia and Her King of kings were in vain.

The scope of the present volume, on the other hand, does not allow us the freehand to dwell on such and may be, if necessary, addressed in another work, should the real need to do so arise in the future.

What does concern us here is a brief introductory presentation of THE REVISED AMHARIC BIBLE OF H.I.M. HAILE SELASSIE I and its relevance to the Rastafarian movement and Ethiopian biblical and pre-Masoretic Hebrew studies. Therefore, we are very grateful to the Ethiopic discoveries and linguistic research that the nineteenth and twentieth centuries have given us through the names of Isenberg, Dillmann and Ullendorff. There were other [European linguists] whom we have neglected to mention whose works are outside of our present scope and contribute little to our present volume.

Yet, there are some whom we cannot, with a clear conscience, ignore or fail to mention. Even in the dawn of the twenty-first century, there are still several modern scholars, researchers and Ethiopic publishers that must be mentioned in these pages, and a volume such as this devoted to THE REVISED AMHARIC BIBLE OF H.I.M. HAILE SELASSIE I, namely Lapsley/Brooks Foundation with a special note to Mr. Bob Lapsley, who has published many rare Ethiopian biblical manuscripts, Christian related books and various other documents, of a spiritual nature, inclusive of, and with an emphasis on the first Amharic New Testament Diaglott, Book of Proverbs and Psalms of David, all based upon the official and Imperial authorized Amharic translation of the HAILE SELASSIE I REVISED AMHARIC BIBLE 1961/62 MSS.

Mr. Lapsley, along with a Dirk Röckmann were responsible, it seems, for the Amharic digitalization of the HAILE SELASSIE I REVISED AMHARIC BIBLE 1961/62 MSS. However, as Mr. Lapsley notes on the acknowledgement page of his Amharic NT Diaglott, the Psalms and Book of Proverbs that, "Heruy Tsigge and his wife Hirut originally entered the texts into the computer, Mulatu Assefa and his wife Misrach Beqele who assisted in the proof reading. Also, we are indebted to Aweqe Mulugeta and Tifsiht Lemma for their encouragement and advice." All of this was accomplished in and about 1992/93, with the blessing and support of the Ethiopian Bible Society along with Ato Kebede Mamo, the said Society's Director.

As we have repeatedly made much mention of, as our hope and firm expectation, by the Grace of the Almighty, to focus our concerted efforts and diligent attention to, along with others who may desire to promote and advance the study of this [Revised] Amharic Bible, along with its distribution, religious and spiritual usage, and, overall, the faithful [Orthodox] Christian based and Rastafarian research of His Imperial Majesty's 1961 Authorized [Revised] Amharic Bible. Furthermore, a development of a companion edition volume, a sort of "Amharic Bible Concordance" along with an Amharic Biblical Etymology will assist the present and future generations, in the diligent and proper comprehension of the many of the unique usages of archaic Ethiopic and Hebraic vocabulary words and phrases, Hebraic and Amharic idioms, Semitic based grammar decoding the inexplicable wordings found in the various ancient MSS and cryptic and Apocryphal biblical texts.

Such a detailed work, no doubt, would require more reliable resources and a host of devoted co-labourers than are currently available to us at the present. It is intended that this present volume will inspire and motive a new generation of interest and fellowship studies within the Society and amongst Rastafari, in particular, and Ethiopian-Hebrews more broadly. Nevertheless, these various notes that have been, and many more that still are being, compiled in the making of this document, it is hoped, may be published in another follow-up edition after this publication is completed – if God so wills.

From what we know, the young Ethiopian-Hebrew prince, RAS TAFARI MAKONNEN, took a keen interest in the preservation and dissemination of Ethiopian biblical and Christian literature, manuscripts and texts prior to His coronation as NEGUSE NAGAST, or "King of kings" of Ethiopia. He purchased the first modern printing press from Europe – where the press was recently invented – into Ethiopia and immediately set out to translate various Ethiopic [Orthodox] church documents, such as liturgies, anaphoras and homilies from Ethiopic [GE'EZ], the old liturgical language, to the Amharic; "from our ancient language into the language which the old and the young understood and spoke."

The name of His Majesty's official press was appropiately christened the "Light and Peace," or the ብርሃንና ሰላም ማተሚያ ቤት BERHANNINA SELAM printing press. It was both works of religious, or a spiritual nature as well as secular, or governmental documents that were published by H.I.H. RAS TAFARI MAKONNEN, crown prince, heir and pleni-potentiary. More details about the printing press and these early translations of RAS TAFARI were documented in Ullendorff's Amharic Chrestomathy.

It was such a printing press that printed a version, that is out of Africa, or – out of Ethiopia, that I discovered, and its not the King James Version. It is in a new, or a renewed and purified – a pure language, the royal [Shoan] Amharic of the "King of Kings of Ethiopia," the prophecied 'Lion of the Tribe of Judah.' But, how is this 'pure language[12]' regarded by the scholars, bibliolators and academics of institutionalized 'white supremacy'? And, is Amharic and the H.I.M. Bible really the missing link in the Biblical story containing the key to the mystery of 'God in Christ'? If Rome represents Mystery Babylon, especially by way of 'Romanism,' in word and in deed – then Ethiopia, particularly the Ethiopia of His Majesty represents the opposite pole of the spiritual reality, or the *Mystery* Zion.

This *Mystery* Zion, or better – the ancient mysteries of Zion, being found and recovered in the African Zion is a fact well attested to and only denied by those who would have at one time believed the world was flat and the sun revolved around the earth. Only Romanism has fostered such bad faith and denied the science that proved their forced conversion to be a perversion of the True Faith. However, to discover that there is an African Zion, true and faithful Ethiopia, the place that the was connected with the Eden and the

---

[12] Refer to Zephaniah Chapter 3, verses 9-10 for a fuller reference to the pure language, Ethiopia and the *Amharic*.

river that came out of her to water the 'garden' should not surprise us, for the Bible tells us so and modern science is continually providing proof to these truths. Yet, if we accept that fact, then the fact that there is a version of the Ancient and Holy Writ that is not the King James Version, must not surprise us either. But, there is more that needs to be disseminated concerning this aspect of our Divine Heritage. In the following section we will attempt to build, ever so gradually and carefully, on this precious foundation, the sure foundation As it is written,

CORINTHIANS CHAPTER 3, VERSE 11

የእግዚአብሔር ጸጋ እንደ ተሰጠኝ መጠን እንደ ብልሃተኛ የአናጺ አለቃ መሠረትን መሠረትሁ፤ ሌላውም በላዩ ያንጻል። እያንዳንዱ ግን በእርሱ ላይ እንዴት እንዲያንጽ ይጠንቀቅ። ከተመሠረተው በቀር ማንም ሌላ መሠረት ሊመሠርት አይችልምና፤ እርሱም ኢየሱስ ክርስቶስ ነው። "According to the grace of God which is given unto me, as a wise masterbuilder, I have laid the foundation, and another buildeth thereon. But let every man take heed how he buildeth thereupon. For other foundation can no man lay than that is laid, which is JESUS CHRIST."

"I discovered a version, that's not the King James Version... for out of Africa came the Garden of Eden."

A few may regard the Amharic language, and the Amharic Bible translations by extension, to be far too young to shed any significant light on any ancient knowledge, biblically speaking. This, sadly, has severely limited and biased the scope of the majority of serious scriptural research into, and any – if not all – or, most of the diligent Biblical scholarship on it to this very date.

Nevertheless, the reggae band, "Steel Pulse" composed and recorded a song entitled, "Not the King James Version" in which the Rastafarian Psalmists sung that: *"I discovered a version, that's not the King James Version... for out of Africa came the Garden of Eden."* That testimony is both factually based; being true and faithful. The question that had come to our attention, more than once, was whether or not these British-based RASTAFARI had H.I.M. HAILE SELLASSIE I'S 1961 AD AUTHORIZED REVISED AMHARIC BIBLE in heart and mind?! No doubt – we did – once we heard the lyrics and the matter became clearer to us by meditation and *"head-resting with and in Jah."* It would thus seem equally appropriate that this essay on the said subject matter should, at least in spirit and truth, attempt to prove that His Majesty's Amharic Bible, often called the [Ethiopian] Emperor's Bible, is by far, a superior and accurate version, in its content, style and authenticity, especially when critically compared with the infamous King of Great Britain, France,

43

and Ireland's KJV 1611 AD edition; one that was published with much pomp and grandeur, but read by only very few. Nevertheless, the King James Version of the Holy Bible provides us presently, and will, in these further essays – a vital and valuable reference point, especially for the majority of English-based readers who may be interested in the claims of the Emperor's bible, THE LION OF THE TRIBE OF JUDAH'S prophetic – "Book of the Seven Seals." REVELATION CHAPTER 5, VERSE 5.

The above New Testament verse from the Book of the Revelation of St. John attained "great prominence in Ethiopia," according to Edward Ullendorff, on page 11, of the Introduction to his otherwise scholarly "Ethiopia and the Bible" – the Schweich Lectures; even though he, like other European scholars of his time, was of the faulty opinion that the heraldic device, that of the Lion of the Tribe of Judah, was of a relatively recent origin in biblical Ethiopia. The fact that Ethiopia's biblical connection precedes even the birth of the Roman Empire is sufficient in and of itself to disprove that the Ethiopians waited for and then resorted to the European heraldic emblems instead of *vis-versa*. Nevertheless, Ullendorff does manage to note the significant biblical reference and symbology, that is in Revelation 5:5 and Imperial Ethiopia: "'No man in heaven, nor in earth' had been found worthy to open the book 'sealed with seven seals.' Finally, one of the elders comforted St. John saying: 'Weep not: Behold, the Lion of the tribe of Judah, the Root of David, hath prevailed to open the book and to loose the seven seals thereof.' The idea of the lion of Judah is, of course, as old as Genesis 49:9, but its application to the royal house of Ethiopia, as part of the Imperial styles, is no great antiquity. The phrase does not occur in the Kebra Nagast, although in chapter 107 the relevant passage from Genesis 49:8-10 in extenso together with suitable embellishments."

What the distinguished Mr. Ullendorff says here concerning the supposed recent usage of the "Lion of the Tribe of Judah" title and its application to the 'royal house of Ethiopia' is quite debatable. He does accurately state that, "of course, [it is] as old as Genesis 49:9" and no doubt it must be recalled that "Ethiopia," or "[the land of the] Cush" is mentioned 47 chapters before in the second Chapter of the Book of Genesis. To add to that point of reference, the symbol of the "Lion" in connection with royalty, nobility and usage in heraldry goes to the very "Natural Genesis" – as Gerald Massey's volumes proves beyond a shadow of a doubt. Thus, the Bible and the Nile Valley civilizations, such as Egypt, both lower and upper has already been referred by other researchers as being, from its very start – a colony of the ancient Ethiopians of antiquity, who have been discovered by this author to originally be called TOBIA, instead of "Ethiopia" and the people therefore, the *Tobiyans* [land of Tob; see Judges 11:3, 5] rather than 'Ethiopians.' This fact in and of itself dismisses

45

significantly the pseudo-Greek origins, a popular fiction that has been and still is erroneously proposed for the classical name of the African roof top country "ÆTHIOPIA." Inclusive of that, the very *African Lion*, or ANBESSA mentioned in the Holy Scriptures has been used as a symbol, an icon of such regal dignity or kingship prior to the FIVE BOOKS OF MOSES called the PENTATEUCH. Thus it is said that, "the Lion is the King of Beasts," and the "Lion is the King of the Jungle." Therefore, in Africa and in Western Asia, encompassing the biblical *Abrahamic* promised lands mentioned in Genesis 15:18, the Lion-King as symbology, according to the mythology of the ancient peoples, almost always refers to the nobility and power of the "Chief Ruler" and "God-King" according to type and motif. The rightful ruler is: THE LION OF THE TRIBE OF JUDAH.

However, we will not belabour the point much more here and do not intent to go much further on it, presently; nor into the curious issue of whether or not the application and heraldic usage of the "LION OF THE TRIBE OF JUDAH" is of relatively recent or remotely antiquated origins in respect to the Imperial Ethiopian house [of David] and the SOLOMONIC Dynasty that sprang from Great King David and subsequently rooted itself firmly in the native soil of the mountainous highlands through the union of King Solomon, the King of Israel and the Queen of Sheba's only son MENYELEK –

as these facts have been thoroughly explored and fully exposited elsewhere.

Even if the "LION OF THE TRIBE OF JUDAH" as heraldry were recently ascribed and applied – the essential matter is that of prophecy and fulfillment in and through His Imperial Majesty, Emperor HAILE SELLASSIE I in light of His prevailing "to open the book and to loose the seven seals thereof."

Ullendorff's assertion to the effect that the phraseology does "not occur in the Kebra Nagast," is of interest because the he continues to explain that, "in chapter 107 the relevant passage from Genesis 49:8-10 *in extenso* together with suitable embellishments." This, when taken from an historical-biblical perspective would definitely indicate that the internal evidence of the document is pre-New Testament, rather than post. It was clearly noted in the version preserved for posterity by the Ethiopian Yesehaq, the Nibura-Id of Aksum, who is rightly accredited with the present composition of the Ethiopic text of the Kebra Nagast in and around roughly the 15th century. The document that has been duly translated into English and entitled as the "Glory of the Kings" contains its own "pearl of great price" – the inherent internal evidence and affirmative claim of authenticity dating from the time of the King of Israel, King Solomon and Queen Makeda of Sabo [Sheba] – even though, as many European scholars and related researchers would feign to late date based upon presumptive conclusions on the relative age of the respective parchments and manuscripts they have appropriated, by various means. Some of these, more recently recovered in Abyssinia, or at least, attributed to the general time period of Solomonic KING ZARA YA'IQOB (1434 - 1468 AD) have been dated and thought to be either copies of foreign origins, or the oldest extant. What is not considered is that unlike Egypt, Ethiopia is a an equatorial country with heavy rainy season in which parchment scrolls would of necessity have to be recopied and rewritten, from generation to generation. Therefore, when a scribe copied an older scroll, in order to preserve and transmit the ancestral wisdom, mainly their name or the relative date or reign of the then ruler would be attached with the earlier version being buried or discarded in some secret or holy place. Besides this, during the Turkish backed MUHAMMADAN, religious war, or "Jihad" – largely composed of the former "Gallas," or the non-Amhara, non-Christian tribalists, pseudo-MUHAMMADAN Oromos coupled with the Osmalis from the North, or Habashistan and the Somalian MUHAMMADAN invasions from the Eastern Horn of Africa. The tip of the pseudo-Islamic ""Jihad" was the 16th century Ahmed Graň, the left-handed, who raged against the throne of David, penetrating deep into the AFRICAN ZION, attacking the heart of the [ተዋሕዶ Tewahədo] Christian and the central Amhara highlands. Due to this devastation of the recent past, many countless monasteries and Ethiopian Orthodox churches, both repositories and venerable storehouses containing various ancient scrolls, parchments, MSS, rare art and facts were intentionally plundered and destroyed by the enemies of the true faith [ርቱዕ ሃይማኖት RƏT'IT HAYMANOT]. Now these documents of antiquity, many preserved for centuries are lost, for the most part, to posterity. Most of the scrolls, parchments or *bərana* and Ethiopic MSS had to be reconstituted, recopied, rewritten, or copied from other churches whom were spared, more or less, and translated again from either Coptic, Arabic, Syriac and even the archaic Hebrew, i.e. ancient Ethiopic that many of the faithful Beta Israel preserved in their communities from the time of Menyelek I. These were mainly the Old Testament and many other Apocryphal works known to both the ancient Ethiopian [Tewahədo] Christians as well as the Black Jews of Ethiopia.

How old or ancient is the original form of the the famous Ethiopian work, the "KEBRA NAGAST", i.e. the "Glory of the Kings [of ETHIOPIA]"?

In his excellent first and second editions of his English translation of the Ethiopic MSS, Sir E.A. Wallis Budge, the distinguished "sometime

Scholar of Christ's College, Cambridge Tyrwhitt Hebrew Scholar, and Keeper of the Department of Egyptian and Assyrian Antiquities in the British Museum," made this important note concerning the document in question, namely that, "[T]his work has been held in peculiar honour in ABYSSINIA [i.e. Ethiopia] for several centuries, and throughout that country it has been, and still is, venerated by the people as containing the final proof of their descent from the Hebrew Patriarchs, and of the kinship of their kings of the Solomonic line with CHRIST, the Son of God."

Mr. Budge, it appears, like many others – DILLMANN, TRUMP, ZOTENBERG, WRIGHT, and BEZOLD – held the later date belief concerning the origins of the Kebra Nagast, namely that it was of fairly recent composition and that it represents a compilation of "the traditions that were current in SYRIA, PALESTINE, ARABIA, and EGYPT during the first four centuries of the Christian era." This theory may account for, what this author considers to be, the second, or New Testament related portions or recessions to the first part – the core contents of what may be termed the Ethiopic Talmud, a type of Book of Chronicles of the Beta Israelites – the transplanted 1,000 princes of the 12 tribes remnant that accompanied Dawit II, known to us as Menyelek I, into

Ethiopia, to "renew the Kingdom of David" as chapter 92, aptly subtitled - *How they renewed the kingdom of* DAVID quite accurately recounts and, for our purposes of history and testimony, recalls in much detail.

Therefore, to ascribe a date to the core, or original elements of the Kebra Nagast to even the fourth century, only takes into account the New Testament, or Christological contents. But, we should not neglect or become willingly ignorant of the fact that, to some degree Mr. Budge was able to hone in upon and highlight, that the foundation of the document is 10th century Before Christ [B.C.] – the roots of the story, or better, our Ethiopic history, is that of the "The Queen of Sheba & Her Only Son Menyelek," as Budge himself re-entitled it – and this also goes far to proves that its oldest *genesis* are definitively in the Old Testament dispensation[13].

Clearly, the KEBRA NAGAST, based upon its older, or rather oldest elements, cannot be limited to the

---

[13] The colophon or title page of the W.A. Budge translation of the *Kebra Nagast* reads and describes the document as follows: "THE 'BOOK OF THE GLORY OF KINGS' (KEBRA NAGAST) A WORK WHICH IS ALIKE THE TRADITIONAL HISTORY OF THE ESTABLISHMENT OF THE RELIGION OF THE HEBREWS IN ETHIOPIA, AND THE PATENT OF SOVEREIGNTY WHICH IS NOW UNIVERSALLY ACCEPTED IN ABYSSINIA AS THE SYMBOL OF THE DIVINE AUTHORITY TO RULE WHICH THE KINGS OF THE SOLOMONIC LINE CLAIMED TO HAVE RECEIVED THROUGH THEIR DESCENT FROM THE HOUSE OF DAVID.
"

late daters and their 4th century speculation. As we have briefly observed, the Kebra Nagast contains not only a post New Testament reference, or rather, as others have alleged – of a late 15th or 16th century scribe or compiler, without any prior antecedent(s). It does not, as "Ethiopia and the Bible," speculates very generally in a cursory manner, have included the more exact phrasing found in REVELATION 5:5; that Mr. Ullendorff and his Semitic scholars and contemporaries seem to allude vaguely to when he writes in reference to the "…Lion of the Tribe of Judah" phraseology and Imperial Ethiopian heraldry, stating thus, that "[T]he phrase does not occur in the KEBRA NAGAST, although in Chapter 107 the relevant passage from Genesis 49:8-10 *in extenso* together with suitable embellishments."

There are two matters that we would like to make a brief commentary of here. Firstly, the latin phrase, *in extenso* means, "at [a] stretch," to say academically and refers to in literary or critical terms, simply speaking, "at full length." This is important in a few ways, as Ullendorff adds furthermore, "together with suitable embellishments" when attempting to link the MOA ANBESSA ZE IMNEGEDE YEHUDA (Conquering Lion of the Tribe of Judah), or dissemble the same with reference to the royal house of Ethiopia. Therefore, we should, or rather must also look at all this, *in extenso*, and find out for ourselves what Mr. Ullendorff, shrewdly and wisely terms as "suitable embellishments" actually are.

From Chapter 107 of the KEBRA NAGAST as translated by Sir E.A. Wallis Budge in his Queen of Sheba and Her only Son Menyelek reads as follows:

Thus JACOB the son of ISAAC prophesied and said, "JUDAH, thy brethren have praised thee. Thine hand is upon the back of thine enemy, and the children of thy mother shall worship thee. And the dominion p. 210 shall not diminish from JUDAH, and the government shall not depart from his kin, until he shall find Him Who hath been waited for, and Who is the Hope of the nations."[1] And he also prophesied and said, "His teeth are white as with snow, and His eyes are glad as with wine, and He shall wash His apparel in wine and His tunic in the blood of clusters of grapes."[2] And again he prophesied, saying, "JUDAH is a lion's whelp; thou hast lain down, and thou hast slept; no one shall wake him up except him that hunteth until he findeth him; rise up from thy strong place."[3] And again JACOB blessed his son JUDAH, and said unto him, "There is a King who shall go forth from thee and shall wash His apparel in wine, and glorious is the place of rest of the Beloved"; now, by "Beloved" CHRIST is meant, and by "Messiah" CHRIST is meant, and JESUS meaneth "Saviour of the people". Now the Prophets mention CHRIST under a secret name and they call Him "the Beloved."

Above is the full quoted passage from Chapter 107 of the KEBRA NAGAST, or "The Queen of Sheba & Her Only Son MENYELEK" – translated for our usage here by Sir E.A. Wallis Budge and referred to by Mr. Ullendorff in his "Ethiopia and the Bible." Ullendorff minces carefully, and weights his words, cleverly and astutely defers to the Genesis Chapter 49 passage concerning the discussion of the "Lion of the Tribe of Judah," in

the opinion of this author, as a way of agreeing somewhat, and also disagreeing somewhat. He attempts to leave open the door to the possibility while not contradicting, at least not overtly, the predominant European scholarship of his time. Thus, as it is said – the jury has remained hung, as it were – in deliberation. The judge must call them in again and ask them if they have come to a decision. *De jure* or *De facto*?

Just imagine: If, indeed the Imperial house of Ethiopia is indeed representative, in spirit and in truth, of the prophesied Messiah-Prince, or "Christ in His Kingly character" – what would the implication be for the Anglo-American and Eurocentric world, of that time, and this, really be? No doubt this and similar questions occupied the hearts and minds of many of these scholars as they poured over and perused these Ethiopic MSS, such as the KEBRA NAGAST; and especially in due consideration of the Conquering Lion of the Tribe of Judah: H.I.M. HAILE SELLASSIE I'S Solomonic claims, namely:

IMPERIAL CONSTITUTION OF ETHIOPIA – ARTICLE II

"The Imperial dignity shall be perpetually attached to the line of HAILE SELASSIE I, descendant of KING SAHLE SELASSIE, whose line descends without interruption from the dynasty of MENELIK I, Son of the QUEEN OF SHEBA, and KING SOLOMON of Jerusalem."

ሞአ፡ አንበሳ፡ ዘአምነገደ፡ ይሁዳ፡

MOA ANBESSA ZE IMNEGEDE YEHUDA

፩፡ የ፡፡ወይበሏ፤፡አሐይ፡እምውስተ፡እልክቱ፡ሊቃናት፡አት
     ብኪ፡ናሁ፡ሞአ፡አንበሳ፡ዘአምነገደ፡ይሁዳ፡ዘአምወስለ
     ት፡ዳዊው፡ለይፃት፡ከመ፡ይፌትሕ፡ለይአቲ፡መጽሐፈ፡
፪፡ ወለማሕተማ፤፡፡ወርእኩ፡ማእከለ፡ዝኩ፡መንበር፡ወ

PROPHECY FULFILLED!

Yet, one must contemplate, and then recall that these very scholars did not, or do not allow – into *their* European *racial* bias right-brained thoughts to intrude upon their left-brained analytical ponderings very often. Good judgment, however, is about the balance of the scales. We must utilize all of our God-given senses, and both aspects of mind, left and right – in harmony and balance; giving each its due honour and service accordingly.

Nevertheless, it would appear that Ullendorff was inclined to favour the Ethiopian Imperial claims, yet is overly cautious, because of his fellow schoolmates of their school of thought, to outrightly and directly say so. Instead, he allows the evidence, so gathered, to speak for itself. Therefore, we still highly regard Mr. Edward Ullendorff and his scholarship in these matters, but – for our part – must go one step further in coming to a more summary judgment of the case that has been left without conclusive decision. Thus, we often make mention of, the ""half of the

55

story," that has not been told, yet must be as the time and opportunity allows us all to do our part.

"For my part, I glory in the Bible." – the Testimony of the Conquering Lion of the Tribe of Judah: H.I.M. HAILE SELLASSIE I.

Rightly, therefore, the KEBRA NAGAST, when weighed in the balance, is thoroughly based upon Old Testament prophetical roots and traditions, and is not merely a New Testament creation of patriotic Ethiopian scribes, as many – such as Mr. Budge – and others have wrongly inferred and vainly speculated and led many to believe. Still, Mr. Budge is to be greatly credited for his manifold efforts, although his own knowledge of Ethiopian history, chronology and related matters, above and beyond many of his own contemporaries, sadly, exhibited curious defects – some, no doubt, due to his own British patriotism, i.e. many of his conclusions were, in the main prematurely biased and largely defective in the main concerning Imperial Ethiopia's rightful heritage as being antecedent to the European heritage and thusly true and authentic. In his voluminous works on Ancient Egypt, when compared to ancient Ethiopia, this bias is glaringly displayed. He seemed to be of the delusion and false opinion that the Nile river flowed from North to South, rather than its true orientation. Budge pretends that the ancient Abyssinians, or better – the Ethiopians – copied slavishly from the later Egyptian culture, instead of being her very Mother, or primogenitor in the remotest antiquity.

The proof of the entire matter, succinctly put, especially when it properly – in character and context – comprehended and received, is the true faith, or Ethiopic Christianity, i.e. TEWAHƏDO, manifested in the person of the Conquering Lion of the Tribe of Judah: H.I.M. HAILE SELLASSIE I, who by virtue of word and deed, is revealed being both the "root of David" [i.e. Ethiopic Judaism] and its very "offspring." ISAIAH CHAPTER 61, VERSE 9; REVELATION CHAPTER 22, VERSE 16.

In conclusion here therefore, what are we to make of Ullendorff's earlier statements? He wisely adds, as an academic effort to hedge his own assumptions, even including a fuller *nota bena* – a direct reference quoted already and to be found in Chapter 107 of the "Glory of the Kings," along with what he terms, "the relevant passage from Genesis 49:8-10 *in extenso* together with suitable embellishments." We must, by all evidence and fact available conclude that all this provides us indeed an even firmer ground, the very "granite and strong foundations" for building up the legitimacy of the Imperial Ethiopian claims – bottoming out the entire matter *"in the beginning,"* or better – the Book of Genesis to its ultimate fulfillment in the Book of Revelation and the unveiling of the "Root of David" in the person of our ""King of kings" [of Ethiopia] – H.I.M. HAILE SELLASSIE I, THE ELECT OF GOD.

This axiomatically – vis-à-vis – leads us to another important prophetic conclusion, that is – the honorific title of the Imperial Ethiopian Sovereign, and that being, "the blessed and only potentate, the King of kings" 1st Timothy Chapter 6, Verse 15. Our Anointed, hence *Christened* "King of kings," or according to the Ethiopic, the ንጉሠ ነገሥት Nəgusä nägäst, – the Emperor of Imperial Ethiopia. The matter here concerns itself with the "appearing of our Lord Jesus Christ: Which in his times shall shew, who is the blessed and only Potentate, the King of kings, and Lord of lords;" – Christ in his 'Second Advent.'

It has been said often by many that although several former kings of Aksum [anglicized as "Axum" elsewhere] also used this royal style and imperial titling. They remind us that it was not until the restoration of the official Solomonic dynasty under YEKUNO AMLAK (1270 – 1285 AD), that the rulers of Imperial Ethiopia generally used the general style of Negus. However, that is only an attempt to explain away the obvious, that is, as far back as the true "first Christian Emperor," King EZANA[14] of Ethiopia –

---

[14] C. 333 AD. It is held that in response to Abba Salama, King Ezana declared Christianity the "state religion" in and about 333 AD. Around this same time, the Roman Empire was alleged to have also converted to a form of "Christianity" during the reign of Constantine.

the Nəgusä nägäst or "King of Kings" appellation has been used as the full title of the Emperor of Imperial Ethiopia.

Is has been alleged and repeatedly said, by some that such other terms such as አጼ ATSÊ (actually a Gondar title for "King" and later used synonymously as Emperor, or Sovereign ruler), ንጉሡ ነገሥት NEGUSE NEGEST (King of kings), and also ሥዩመ እግዚአብሔር SEYOUME IGZIABEHER (meaning the Elect or Appointed of God) were ascribe and used for the Ethiopian Emperors. This is more or less true generally but the matter at hand is to establish in this written document that His Imperial Majesty Haile Selassie I fulfills the "Lion of the Tribe of Judah" prophecy not only because of His Imperial title, but because of His Divine ability to be the Only One able with such an anointing and carrying such a high and heavenly responsibility of government upon His shoulder to "open the book, and to loose the seven seals thereof" – as it is written in the BOOK OF REVELATION OF ST. JOHN the Divine scribe.

Thus it is not only the title but it is the deed done by the proper and worthy one who was able to accomplish it that we are concerned with at this point. Anyone may have or claim a title. The question would then be: Are they worthy? And, if so: Are they able to do the written deed? In both of these cases we are convinced and convicted that yes, He who is H.I.M. – His Imperial

Majesty is both worthy and His *Revised Amharic Bible* becometh the proof positive that He did that which was written of Him, namely that He is the "Christ [lit. Anointed One] in His [Davidic] Kingly character."

Whether we say "Davidic" or "Solomonic" it is a matter of references to relative points of origin. King Solomon was the "worthy" son of King David and the Kebra Nagast, in Chapter 92 speaks of *"How they renewed the kingdom of DAVID"* in the highland of Abyssinia – biblical Ethiopia. Yet, "David" is the key and 'cornerstone' of the biblical symbolism in both the old and the New Testament as concerning "the glorious kingdom of Christ" and the rightful authority of rulership. The Seventh of the biblical covenants is termed the "Davidic Covenant" – 2nd Samuel Chapter 7:4-17; 1st Chronicles Chapter 17:4-17. This covenant is a fourfold one that secures the following, namely:

1. A Davidic *"House*[15]*"*; i.e. posterity, family.

2. A *"Throne"*; i.e. royal authority.

3. A Kingdom, i.e. sphere of rule, or *"Imperial Domain"* [by extension – an Empire]

4. In perpetuity; *"for ever."*

---

[15] Or, a Household, by extension in Biblical usage – a church; or, further in the sense of the Ethiopian World Federation, a local; thus the reference made in the historic EWF preamble to the Constitution and By-Laws to the phraseology – 'our divine heritage.'

Upon this ancient and Holy covenant, the Davidic Covenant *specifically*, that the glorious kingdom of THE CHRIST, "of the Seed of David according to the flesh" was and is to be truly founded and recovered, both then and now. The covenant, like the cross of Christ, is fourfold one and it has only one conditional clause, and that is: **disobedience in the Davidic family brings the Visitation of chastisement but not an abrogation of the Covenant,** or any part thereof. Judgment in the family of God, is always remedial, not penal. However, with the wicked – it is penal, not remedial. This has been referenced by a noteworthy Dr. C.I. Scofield in his highly recommended English language and KJV based, *First Scofield Study Bible*[16].

The term "Solomonic" must be understood in this sense, that being the renewal of "the kingdom of David." The mystical Father-Son relationship here and elsewhere in our story of the Bible is both prophetical scripturally and mythologically significant and symbolic when rightly comprehended from the "Book of the Beginnings."

Now the Imperial heraldry and title of MOA ANBESSA ZE IMNEGEDE YEHUDA (Conquering Lion of the Tribe of Judah) – which is the exact Ethiopic or GE'EZ rendering of "the Lion of the

---

[16] Based upon the 1909 edition of the Scofield Reference Bible

Tribe of Judah hath prevailed," as found in Revelation Chapter 5, Verse 5.

MOA ANBESSA ZE IMNEGEDE YEHUDA

ሞአ : አንበሳ : ዘእምነገደ : ይሁዳ :

Conquering Lion of the Tribe of Judah,

Or,

"THE LION OF THE TRIBE OF JUDAH HATH PREVAILED"

፭፤ የ።ወይቤለኒ፡አሐዱ፡እምውተት፡አልእቱ፡ሊቃናት፡አኀ ሥነኪ፡ናሁ፡ሞአ፡አንበሳ፡ዘእምነገደ፡ይሁዳ፡ዘእምወስ ተ፡ሥርው፡ለዳዊት፡ከመ፡ይፈትሕ፡ለይእቲ፡መጽሐፈ፡ ፮፤ ወለማኅተማሃ።ወርኢኩ፡ማእከለ፡ዝኩ፡መንበር፡ወ

Ethiopic text taken from NOVUM TESTAMENTUM DOMINI NOSTRI ET SERVATORIS JESU CHRISTI AETHIOPICE edited by Thomas Platt, 1830.

It has been said that the significant phrase, namely, MOA ANBESSA ZE IMNEGEDE YEHUDA (Conquering Lion of the Tribe of Judah) – has always preceded the Imperial title of the *rightful* Ethiopian Emperors. Nevertheless, it was not a personal title, but rather was to refer to the title of THE CHRIST, i.e. "the Lord's Anointed" or the MESSIAH. The placement of such meant that the Christ was ahead of, or, *on* the Head of the duly chosen, anointed and crowned "King of kings," or Emperor's throne name, symbolizing an act of the Imperial submission to the primacy of the "SON OF GOD," i.e. JESUS OF NAZARETH.

Until the time of Yohannes IV, the Emperor of Ethiopia was also called the NEGUSE TSION (King of Zion). NƏGUSÄ NÄGÄST, or "Emperor" was also entitled to the dignities of being referred to in speech and writing as GIRMAWI (His/Your Imperial Majesty), as well as JANHOY (somewhat the equivalent of the English "Sire"; although, according to this author, there is to be found a Semitic etymological link in the Ethiopic term with Hebraic "ADONAI" that is most interesting and may be noted elsewhere). The Gondarine royal title of ATSE was not originally used by the Southern SHOAN [SHEWAN] rulers – post YEKUNO AMLAK, as was noted by Revd. C.W. Isenberg in his two part volume of his excellent Dictionary of the Amharic Language, pg 15, filed under the older ሐፄ HÂTZÊ form instead of አጼ ATSÊ. *On the other hand,* አጼ ATSÊ has been used for the Nəgusä nägäst [Emperor] when being referred to in the third person, and not directly. Also, in his own household and amongst the intimate family, He – the *Nəgusä nägäst,* may be called upon with due honours as GETOCHU (an Amharic term literally meaning "the Masters" – very much like the plural ADONAI instead of ADONI; and taken to mean "our Master" in the plural or formal sense of the word).

Thus, one language or spoken dialect may be modified or even change in generations and overtime, however, with the Hebraic, coming from its Ethiopic [archaic GE'EZ] roots produces another form, or a 'new tongue' called Amharic.

However, what remains the same is the cultural pattern, or 'way of life' that is regulated amongst the chosen people by the Holy covenant. Therefore, whether አዶናይ *Adonai* was the expression then, in the distant biblical past, the expression ጃንሆይ *Janhoi* reflects the resonance of the same. Yet, within the Amharic, to say 'my saviour,' one may choose አዳኜ *Adāñê*, similar to another word አዳኜ – *Adāñê*, that means a 'hunter, or seeker (of the lost).'[17] These actually points to both Adonai and *Adoni* in morpheme, or by the way it sounds, and the object in relation to the subject and speaker. These etymological connections between the Hamo-Semitic, called elsewhere the Afro-Asiatic and nowadays, by us as the Kamo-Shemitic, will be addressed in other writings based on the related research into the Ethiopic's role as the First Language or the pre-Babel common ancestor tongue by this Author. However, not to go off of the topic and theme at hand, we now will address three more subjects, or background matters that are like 'prerequisites' necessary to the understanding of the H.I.M. Haile Selassie I Amharic Bible in context; and to it truly being the actual "Book of the Seven Seals" (Revelation 5:5) of Judeo-Christian prophecy by our briefly covering the following items in the summary of this present text, namely:

---

[17] A note is in order here, namely – in ancient times a 'saviour' was a type of hunter and a hunter was a mythological type of hero, or ancient saviour.

1. THE NECESSITY OF AN AMHARIC REVISION

2. FROM ABU RUMI TO HIS IMPERIAL MAJESTY

3. THE FIVE (5) MAIN TRANSLATIONS OF THE HOLY BIBLE INTO THE AMHARIC

These are three topical subjects are of prerequisite importance, each in its own turn, and thus must be given due attention by us prior to a more detailed treatment, analysis or commentary on the H.I.M. HAILE SELASSIE I Amharic Bible. A few key questions we will begin to address in these three forthcoming brief chapters are:

What were the versions prior to the publication of the Emperor's Amharic Bible?

What effect did these other versions have, if any, on the Emperor's Amharic Bible?

Why was it necessary to produce an Authorized "Amharic Bible" after the Abu Rumi version?

What were the strengths and the set-backs in the Abu Rumi version due to the foreign European Christian Missionary influence?

What are the Five (5) Main Translations of the Holy Bible into Amharic? And, what was the source and resources used for each?

How does the Emperor's Amharic Bible demonstrate its superiority of authenticity and accuracy by comparison to the Abu Rumi?

Why were the other versions translated either from Arabic-to-Amharic (like the Abu Rumi), or from English-to-Amharic (like the UBS and IBS); while

65

His Majesty's Amharic Bible was instead translated from the Ancient language, i.e. Ethiopic [Ge'ez] and diligently compared with the [Masoretic] Hebrew for the Old Testament and the Koine [LXX Greek] for the New[18]?

Which Amharic Bible translation(s) is most reliable, accurate and trustworthy a translation? And, which ones are not and why?

Why are the United Bible Society (UBS[19]) and the International Bible Society (IBS) suppressing the distribution of the 1961/62 AD Amharic Bible and encouraging their own foreign-based translations?

---

[18] See the Appendix & Endnotes for the translation of His Majesty's Preface to the Revised Amharic Bible published in this manuscript; the Emperor details briefly the process used by His Imperial translators in the accomplishing the great and noteworthy task of producing a uniquely royal Amharic and Ethiopic-based version, all without the religious influences or theological debates [i.e., Protestant vs Romanist] of the foreign-based European missionaries or Anglo-American Christian Bible Societies. This Bible is not only a very good bible, but moreover, it is a work of great literary achievement touching areas of both Education and Fine Arts, i.e. linguistics, poetry, prose, drama and even music [Psalms, Song of Songs & Lamentations].

[19] The UBS has become disappointing as of late in the fact that they who were given the original license to publish the Authorized version in 1962, a year after the initial publication, have since attempted to replace the 'Amharic Bible' by a modern counterfeit that is a recent English-to-Amharic Bible produced by Western Christian missionaries and covert Romanist agents, perhaps Jesuits.

The Necessity of an Amharic Revision

THE NECESSITY OF AN AMHARIC REVISION

The Authorized [Amharic] 1960/61 AD Bible of His Majesty has been ascribed and referred to as the "Revised Amharic Bible." The question before us is simply this: *Was there a need for a revision of Amharic Bible? Was it indeed a Revision of the Abu Rumi Amharic Bible of 1860 AD? (As has been presumed and assumed by other less informed scholars, bibliolators and Ethiopianist writers previously.)*

The French Consul in Cairo, Asselin de Cherville, possessed a manuscript containing a complete translation of the Bible into Amharic, created by the mutual efforts of the Consul and the Ethiopian monk named Abu Rumi (1750 - 1819); or *Abu Romê*. As Ullendorff relates, for ten years "every Tuesday and Saturday his [de Cherville's] door was shut to all visitors when he read with 'my Abyssinian, slowly and with the utmost attention, every verse of the Sacred Volume, in the ArabicVersion which we were able to translate.' But we are not told from which Arabic version the rendering was made." Where the Arabic words were "abstruse, difficult, or foreign," de Cherville then consulted "the Hebrew Original, the Syriac Version, or the Septuagint" for clarification. This is the testimony on record of the French Consul in Cairo, Mr. de Cherville. The Bible that they composed was not based upon Ethiopic or Ge'ez manuscripts, that may have not been available to them in the complete version, perserved in inner Africa, i.e. the Highlands of Ethiopia in a variety of Holy and Sacred indigenous 'Ethiopian Orthodox' Tewahedo Churches and monestaries.

Therefore, the Abu Rumi (አቡ ሩሚ) version, that became the result of the efforts referred to already, was not an authentic or authorized translation nor was it based upon the ancient Ethiopian biblical languages; but was a superimposition of the Arabic version, composed itself from earlier Coptic and perhaps even the Ethiopic version itself. The process used to compiled and translate an 'Ámharic' language Bible by the French Consul, other European Bible Societies and the host of Western Christian Missionaries was the opposite of, and in reverse, or actually an inverse of process or the 'Way' used by the Imperial Translators of the H.I.M. Haile Selassie I Revised Amharic Bible; who translate firstlly by consulting with the ancient Ethiopic scrolls, comparsions with the Hebrew Masoretic, the Septuagint Greek LXX to the archaic Amharic versions and eventually into the Royal vernacular, the language which both the young and old understood and spoke in daily usage by the African Zion, the Kingdom of David, renewed in the Highland of Ethiopia – fulfilling the prophecies of the Holy Bible, particularly Psalms, which testify to the fact that: መዝሙረ ዳዊት 67 (68): 31 መኳንንት ከግብጽ ይመጣሉ ኢ.ትዮጵያ እጆችዋን ወደ እግዚአብሔር ትዘረጋለች፡፡

PSALM OF DAVID 68: 31 "Princes shall come out of Egypt; Ethiopia shall soon stretch out her hands unto GOD."

From Abu Rumi
to
His Imperial Majesty

FROM ABU RUMI TO HIS IMPERIAL MAJESTY

It may be noted that I have presented a somewhat lengthly excurse into the development of the Rastafari movement vis-a-vis the teachings of His Imperial Majesty, however, the origin of the Amharic scholarship of the respective translators of the Amharic Bible, I have concluded, has not be sufficient address and thus have been gradually led into tracing this process a little further in this essay. Overall, this work should be seen as a prolegomena to a study of the Amharic Bible of 1960/61 AD, that is, the Emperor's Bible – the Authorized Revised [Amharic] Version. It is moreover hoped that others may find these preparatory studies useful to clearing the ground for future research coupled with some particular interest in their own right.

I have looked at my task, firstly, but not limited to – writing a brief history of the Amharic Bible translation from 1860 to 1960/61, from the Abu Rumi version to that of the Emperor's, as accurately and succinctly as was possible. This has actually proven to be more of a task than originally thought when all of the relevant detail is assembled and view from the present perspective of the author. Secondly, I had intended to present and confine my textual investigations to a few cursory examples and renderings in the two versions that are separated by almost exactly one hundred years. Besides the texts themselves, there is not much that is currently available that can throw much light on the exact sources, methods or the equipment used by the translators. However, His Majesty is to be credited highly for His Preface, or the Speech concerning the Revised Amharic Bible that gives much more detail about His Bible and the thought, intent and general process employed by His College of translators. Yet, there are critical details that we lack at this time and must be content to analyze what is before us until further research provides us more matter to be scrutinized. Nevertheless, what we do have before us is a wealth of knowledge in the very text of both Amharic versions themselves that are the clearest evidences of the development and considerable improvements that been noted already in "Ethiopia and the Bible." The first chapter entitled "Bible Translations" is a highly recommended reading for any student serious interested in the history and process of the respective translations of the Amharic Bible which we will not rehash at the present for sake of continuing what others such as Ullendorff, admittedly, were unable to do in their time yet provided a basis for further scholarship, research and investigations.

This we will address but first let us review the already established conventional view of the matter by recalling the history of Christianity in Ethiopia. After indigenous Ethiopic Christianity, i.e. Acts of the Apostles Chapter 8 and the Ethiopian "Eunuch" was superceded, rather, dominated by the Egyptian Orthodox introduced by the shipwrecked Tyrian youths and Frumentius, a new form of religion became the prevailing "state religion" of "Abyssinia," thereafter known as Christian 'Ethiopia' in and around the 4th century. This would make the King of kings, King Ezana, as a matter of history and fact, the newly baptized Ethiopian Monarch, the actual first Christian Emperor in the world rather than Constantine of Rome. It is believed that the Bible was first translated into Ge'ez or "Ethiopic," the Ecclesiatical language of the Empire about that time. However, this is inaccurate as the Hebrew or Judaic Ethiopian tradition precedes the alleged conversion from the indigenous religions, erroneous referred to as "paganism," to the new Orthodox [Egyptian Domination] that was introduced at the very same time. Thus, much of the present story of Ethiopia has been interpreted by others who have forced a clear discrepancy of the facts concerning exactly when "Christianity" was brought to Ethiopia and by whom. We have the testimony of His Majesty that echos the very words of the New Testament concerning the Ethiopian Official, called the Eunuch and Treasurer of the Ethiopian Queen Candace. Whether this Candace was "Ethiopian" or "Nubian" has also been and may well continue to be debated in some circles of Academia. However, the fact of the matter is that Africa, and Ethiopia in particular was "introduced" to the Gospel of Our Lord and Saviour Jesus Christ, and by extension – early christianity, well prior to and before the so-called 4th century theory that has been often repeated without due diligence to the written and recorded testimony found in the very sacred pages of the scriptures. The question only remains for those who still have any doubt about the truth in this regard as to whom shall they believe or accept as truthful? For our part, like the Emperor, we are inclined to accept the testimony of the Bible as truth, especially since the antiquity of true indigeous [Ethiopic] Christianity antedates the fourth century version that has become legitimized by repeated repetitions, even sadly, by many of the modern Ethiopian Orthodoxy.

However, be that as it may, the controversy concerning early Ethiopian Christianity, either 1st or 4th century requires further investigation and critical inquiry. This edition has simply attempted to inform the reader that there are discrepancies between the traditions as these bear implications on when the scriptures appeared or were translated into the Ge'ez and by whom they were translated and when. If we would argue from the conventional approach, we would be forced to believe that the Holy Bible was was first translated into the Ethiopic-GE'EZ about the time of the 4th century alleged conversion and establishment of the "state religion" during the reign of the Ethiopian Emperor Ezana. Nevertheless, what is a little more well documented is that "only in the last two centuries [has] appeared Translations of the Bible into Amharic." *Were there other 'Amharic Translations' before His Majesty's Bible? How many were there? Who, or rather – whom were the key figures that were responsible for each of these 'Amharic Translations'?* These are just a few of the questions that we discuss further in the next section that follows immediately this one.

THE FIVE (5) MAIN TRANSLATIONS OF THE HOLY BIBLE INTO THE AMHARIC LANUAGE

The Five (5) Main Translations of the Holy Bible into the Amharic

As of this writing, there are five (5) main Translations of the Bible into the Amharic language that are known to the present author. I am acquainted with each of these five translations and have diligently investigated each in considerable detail. However, this is not our intent here. But it is hoped that a more critical edition may be composed to compare each in its turn, line by line, verse by verse, and even word by word distinguishing the nuances that certain translators used and favoured as opposed to other who chose other expressions. Ullendorff in the first chapter entitled "Bible Translations" of his excellent and well-referenced and annotated introduction into this subject matter, "Ethiopia and the Bible," has given much of the prerequisite history of the linguistic details to be weighed and balanced, by well-prepared scholarship that is sadly lacking and not given due consideration amongst the Academia and institutions devoted to biblical studies.

However, a brief history of the Amharic Bible translation from 1860 to 1960/61 AD is the main focus of my task here as the last two, the UBS Versions (1987, 2005) and the IBS Version (2001), are not really worthy of our serious scholarly consideration at this time, mainly but not only due to the fact that they have been translated largely based upon non-Ethiopic [Ge'ez] texts and MSS. It may be be compared and likened, by example, to translating the KJV or NIV English language versions into the modern colloquial Amharic language or dialectical speech commonly spoken nowadays. Some find these "new," or better ferenj Amharic versions preferrable because of the post-Revolutionary apathy that has cursed the careless Ethiopians and many of this present generation that have been infected; even the young Ethiopian students, scholars and Christian "Orthodox" folk have displayed a tragic and prophetic forgetfulness concerning their own God-given roots and ancient biblical culture. Thus, it is written by the Prophet Jeremiah, who was rescued by the Ethiopian named Ebed-Melech:

JEREMIAH CHAPTER 2, VERSE 14

በዉኑ እስራኤል ባሪያ ነዉን?
ወይስ የቤት ዉላጅ ነዉን?
ስለምን ብዝበዛ ሆነ?

"[Is] Israel a servant?
[Is] he a homeborn [slave]?
Why is he spoiled?"

Even a great majority of the European scholars have lamented the lack of interest and "scholarly attention" given lately to the [Amharic] Bible translations and editions amongst young [Ethiopian] Scholars. Ullendorff had noted that great monuments of "Ethiopian Literature still remains without a proper critical edition.[20]" This volume is a somewhat belated attempt to answer that clarion call to intellectual arms for the defense and dissemination, to a new generation, even a generation yet come – one yet to be born, encouraging them in advance, and preparing the Way for them to continue in the progressive development and fruit-bearing growth of the "Tree of Life,[21]" – the "Book of Life," the repository or treasury of the [divine] knowledge, or γνοσισ *gnosis* of the truth. for it is written, "Ye shall know the truth, and the truth shall set you free.[22]"

The analogies between the "tree" and its by-product, the "book" are numerous in Ethiopic MSS and especially in reference to the Holy Bible[23] in Ethiopic indigenous "Orthodoxy" [or, Tewahedo]. Even in Judaism, when one goes to make aliyah, or going up to read the scrolls of the

---

[20] page 33, *Ethiopia and the Bible*, by Ullendorff.

[21] An interesting side note concerning the "Tree of Life" may be briefly summarize here by reference to Sir E.A. Wallis Budge's 1929 translation of the Ethiopic "LEFAFA SEDEK," interpreted as being the "Bandlet of Righteousness" and euphemistically known as the Ethiopian Book of Life. This ancient book has been speculated as being an Ethiopian version of the ancient Egyptian Per Em Heru, or "Book of the Dead."

[22] St. John Chapter 8, Verse 32

[23] Of added reference is the evidence that The FIRST SECTION contains the SALOT BA'E[NTA] MADKHANIT, *i.e.* the "Prayer for redemption (or salvation)," which is taken from the MASHAFA HAYWAT, *i.e.* the "Book of Life," which is called "LEFAFA SEDEK."

Law, known as the "Torah," the handles of the scroll are called and known as the "tree of life." This metaphor – or "parable" is definitely much older than the Hebrew Genesis and book of Proverbs and Revelation of St. John and likely has its true "Natural Genesis" and *Kamite* origins in the ancestral Wisdom of the Egypts, in which even Moses was said and recorded to have been adept, or a master in "word and deed.[24]"

It was Moses, the one who is called in Ethiopic, Muse – meaning the head of a fraternal order, or "Brotherhood" was learnt in the word, linguistics and language of the ancient Mysteries. These were re-encoded into the "Hebrew" of the Mosaic Age. An important distinction must be made between the "Hebrew" of the time of Moses and the modern forced "Hebrew" – or, Yiddish of the "Jews" of the 'state of [modern] Israel.' It is at this juncture that we must refer to the relevant work of August Dillmann named "Ethiopic Grammar" that has given powerful and accurate testimony to Ethiopic's [Ge'ez] proto-Hebraic origins. When we consider that Moses' father-in-law, Jethro, was an "Ethiopian" and the many other important and significant "Ethiopians" in the holy scripture texts as well as their role in the development and progression of the biblical prophetic idea, it should not surprise any that

---

[24] ACTS OF THE APOSTLES Chapter 7, Verse 22.

there must be an equally significant impact and influence of "Ethiopic" on both the pre-Hebrew Old Testament and the New Testament linguistics. In this regard, William Gesenius and his Hebrew Lexicon makes numerous references to ancient Ethiopic and Ge'ez etymologies in order to clarify the biblical Hebrew meanings and provide modern Judaism with a more authentic point of comparison.

We have felt it necessary to briefly refer to Ullendorff, Dillmann and Gesenius' respective Semitic-based research papers, volumes and books that have left us with a testimony to the intimate relationship between Ethiopic and the biblical Hebrew. Any critical and detail discussion of the Translations of the Bible into Amharic must actually begin with such a retrospect in regards to the Ethiopic scholarship. There are many other scholars that we could and would have liked to comment on in this edition but due to urgency of publication we have had to summarize much of our lengthlier commentaries for other essays and compilations. Those who are inspired to search out the matter for themselves should start with chapter one (Bible Translations) found in Ullendorff's "Ethiopia and the Bible" that gives us the best overview of the prior scholasticism in the field of Ethiopic studies. His footnotes, commentary and annotations are invaluable for the diligent student and should be made use of.

Before we move on to the specifics of the Translations of the Bible into Amharic, let us mention O. Lofgren, another linguist and scholar of some merit, especially in regards to Ethiopic studies and the Ge'ez Bible MSS. was reported by Prof. Ullendorff as having had proposed the "establishment of an international body to organize a critical edition of the Ethiopic Bible" in the mid to late 60s. The initiation of the practical steps to meet this challenge were not able to be implemented or taken at that time. Hopes and expectation were left unfulfilled, even though the challenge still faces us in the present and *ad infinitum*. As O. Lofgren proposed, "The first task of such an institute would be the preparation of all Bible MSS. In Ge'ez known to exist in Europe as well as in Ethiopia" to be followed by the assignment of text editions to individual scholars[25].

We, therefore, give thanks and praises for the present priviledge that we have been afforded both, time and opportunity, as one "individual scholar," a sort of Rastafarian *debtera*[26], who is

---

[25] Ullendorff's additional note based on Professor Lofgren's unpublished paper submitted to the Third International Conference of Ethiopian Studies at Addis Ababa, 1966 AD; pg. 33.

[26] An unordained, highly learned priest, member of the indigenous clergy or educated layperson. A traveling "teacher of righteousness," similar to the Old testament prophet-types who may also serve as an itinerant religious [Christian]

enabled, by learning and experience over 19 years in the study of the Amharic Bible and Ethiopic MSS (or, manuscripts).

History of Translations of the Bible into Amharic

- **1 Abu Rumi translation (1860s)**
- **2 First Haile Selassie I Bible (1935)**
- **3 New Haile Selassie I Bible (1962)**
- **4 UBS Versions (1987, 2005)**
- **5 IBS Version (2001)**

Abu Rumi translation

The first known translation of the Bible into Amharic is said to have been made by Abu Rumi in the early 19th century. In the opinion of Edward Ullendorff, "The history of the first translation of the Bible into Amharic is a romantic and exciting story which deserves to be better known among *éthiopisants*[27]. The fullest account is contained in William Jowett, *Christian Researches in the Mediterranean* (London, 1822); this book has an extremely interesting and valuable on 'Abyssinians', running to some sixty pages." Mr. Jowett is quoted as claiming, 'though

---

teacher in highland Ethiopia; usually well-versed in the Psalms of David, spiritual hymns and poetry – likened to St. Yared. Debteras are considered to be the original type of Muse [Moses], mystics, magicians possessing the ability to create protective amulets and talismans to ward off malevolent spirits.

[27] Ullendorff, *Ethiopia and the Bible: The Schweich Lectures* (Oxford: British Academy, 1968), p. 62

85

the province which beats the name of Amhara is small, its dialect is spoken through at leasr half of Abyssinia' on page 197 of his forementioned 1822 volume.

In this exploration of the Translation of the Bible into Amharic, we have neglected to mention what is known as Archaic Amharic, or true [Ethiopic] – defined roughly as the earliest stage of the dialect derived from the old Ge'ez to what we refer today as modern "Amharic." Most European and other Gentile writers on the subject matter has purposely, and some indeed due to ignorance of the Ethiopic Genesis, have avoided the indigenous nature of the Ethiopic Bible from an Old Testament time. With the natural progression of the people and their identifying with the Solomonic Dynasty, it is not necessary to look to an outside origin for the Bible in Ethiopia, but rather an indigenous or native source that has been claimed by the Kebra Nagast and the tradition interpretation **"ALIKE THE TRADITIONAL HISTORY OF THE ESTABLISHMENT OF THE RELIGION OF THE HEBREWS IN ETHIOPIA.[28]"**

"Some respectable pieces of evidence can be adduced in favour of each hypotheses, but it seems that reality was a good deal more complex and eclectic than is sometimes conceded, and the

---

[28] From E.A. Wallis Budge's 1922 English translation of the Ethiopic Kebra Nagast – "the Book of the Glory of Kings," also known as The Queen of Sheba & Her Only Son Menyelek I.

linguistic facts refuse to fall into neat patterns.[29]" The acknowledgment that "the linguistic facts" concerning the Ethiopic and Amharic indigenous Bible versions, "refuse to fall into neat patterns." The problem and obstacle that has faced and still confronts the majority of [White] Western and Eurocentric scholarship, in regards to Ethiopic studies, is that there has been, and sadly still are, varied attempts by non-Ethiopian pseudo-scholars to either ascribe the origins of the Ethiopic Bible to outside influences, whether Septuagint LXX or the Masoretic recession of the Hebrew OT, or on the other hand, the perpetual habit of late dating of ancient Ethiopic MSS in order to make the true linguistic history of the antiquity of Ethiopic MSS. fit within a "neat pattern" and predetermined point of view that does not significantly challenge or contradict the falsified and unsubstanciated claims of the Aryan school of thought that previously alleged that "Egypt" was not actually on the African continent. This "European madness" expressed to this day by so-called modern European "Jewish" and Western [Gentile] Christian world views continues to deny the [Black] African origins of both Ancient Egypt and the Bible. On the Greek and Septuagint LXX arguments, it can be counter-proposed, with fact and evidence, that many of the original ethnic "[Black] Hebrews" and biblical Israelites were sold to the "children of the Grecians." Thus, who, better than they, could have produced the first Hebrew translation into the early koine koine or common "Greek" language that comprised the earliest and oldest known Septuagint MSS.?

PROPHECY OF JOEL, CHAPTER 3, VERSE 6

ከዳርቻቸውም ታርቄአቸው ዘንድ የይሁዳና የኢየሩሳሌምን ልጆች ለግሪክ ሰዎች ሽጣችኋልና፤

"The Children of Judah (So-called African-American **"Negro"**) And Of Jerusalem Have Ye **Sold To The Grecians** *('Pan-Hellenistic' so-*

---

[29] Ullendorff, *Ethiopia and the Bible: The Schweich Lectures* (Oxford: British Academy, 1968), p. 56

called Black Greeks; The Boule?), That Ye Might Remove Them Far From Their Border (The Promised Land; E. Africa & Middle-East)."

VERSE 8

"And I will sell your (Tyrian, Sidonian and Phoenician) sons and daughters into the hand of the children of Judah, **and they shall sell them to the Sabeans, to a people afar off: for the LORD hath spoken it.**"

The "LORD," or YHWH is speaking against Tyre, Sidon and "all the coasts of Palestine" in a prophetic period of time known as the "the judgment of the Gentile nations after Armageddon" that is usually interpreted to be after the Second Advent, or the second coming of Christ. We will not discuss at this writing the theological implications of this prophecy, according to the Aryan recession and the African original, or "Natural Genesis" of the Hebrew Bible. But what is very clear cut is that the children of Judah whom we may say can be rightly called "Hebrews" will have direct access, communication and trade with the biblical Sabeans. It need only be recalled to mind that the "Queen of the South" is also known as the "Queen of Sheba" and "Sheba" is etymologically, ethnically, linguistically and culturally related to the "Sabeans" or ancient Æthiopians.

Therefore our "**Sold To The Grecians**" theory and the JUDAH-GRECIAN-SABEAN approach that we are hereby introducing, in brief, serve both now and as followed-up by additional critical analysis, to answer many more of the related outstanding, controversial and still unaddressed questions concerning the HEBREW-GREEK-ETHIOPIC linguistics of the Ethiopian Bible. This provides, for now, the best insight into both, the historical as well as untangle the seemingly complex, confusing and sometimes contradictory linguistics behind the Ethiopian translations of the Bible and the various phases of text that have been positively identified. Also the basis for the origin of the ancient polyglot Bible versions, largely traced to the AD period are brought into a better context and perspective for future students of Ethiopic and Amharic Bible studies. The possibilities of the Ethiopic Bible's translation, in the first phase, out of, or at least alongside of, the Septuagint LXX must also be re-evaluated in light of the Prophet Joel's Chapter 3, Verse 6 and Verse 8 prophecies. At the core of this West to East exchange or 'sale' of captives, firstly the Hebrews into Greece, and later, the Greeks to the Sabeans indicate and point to the central role of the "children of Judah" who would represent the Hebrew influence, both linguistically and culturally. In this, Ethiopia become a more likely, no – the best candidate for the repository of the to and fro transactions and inter-exchange of cultural and literary influences, all preserved and fossilized, as it were, in the richness of the Hebrew, Greek, Coptic, Syriac [Arabic?], and

Aramaic influences found naturally blended into the polyglott of the ancient Ethiopic MSS and, curiously also found in the Emperor's [Amharic] Bible text, ancient nomenclature [names], syntax, vocabulary, transliterations, etc.

According to the Prophet Joel's prophecy, the children of Judah would have to have familiar contacts with the Sabaens who undoubtably are either Ethiopians or Abyssinian directly or by direct blood ties and ethnic relations. These connections were known in the Old Testament times in which Prophets like Joel prophecised and were not disputable then (namely because the peoples knew themselves), and therefore should not be entertained now without a sufficient degree of evidence to prove or disprove otherwise. When all of this is taken affirmatively into serious account, especially regarding the Ethiopian's historical testimony as being essentially accurate, i.e. Solomon-Sheba and the "Black Jews of Ethiopia" being lost tribes, the Ethiopian Eunuch etc. it becomes more than evident that there is no complexity, contradiction or confusion about the matter at hand. The ancient Ethiopians spoke the truth about their own Judeo-Christian origins and roots in the Old Testament covenants and relationship with both the "God of ISRAEL" and the ethnic Hebrews themselves. The main reason why this has not been recognized and accepted as a fact is, and cannot be rationalized away otherswise, as being a by-product of the racial bias and intellectual dishonesty of the entrenched European and Anglo-American "Protestant" traditions institutionalized in Academia, the press and throughout the predominantly "white supremacy" complicit media establishment that still refuses to acknowledge the latest rebuttal of the accepted errors of a by-gone "white-washed" sepulchural age when traffic in "[Black] Hebrew slaves" was big business and offended not many of their highminded consciences.

Undue credit has usually been mistakenly given and ascribed, as a matter of fact assumption, to the alleged and undocumented *Ferenj* influences; even in the most ancient traditions, rather than – to the native and indigenous genius, given graciously by the God of Israel to the His chosen Ethiopians in preserving, transmitting and overall maintaining such a rare and ancient archive of rare biblical works of sacred literature, many virtually unknown and unheard of in the West and Europe prior to the past couple of hundreds of years since the Europeans were able to find the "source of the Nile," such as Mr. James Bruce and his celebrated journeys into the highlands of Abyssinia [Ethiopia].

Mr. Bruce is a very interesting character in the 'Abyssinia' discovery from an Anglo-European perspective; but a more detailed analysis of Mr.

Bruce and his 'discoveries' in another volume. From this point we would like to summarize what we have found and can document and prove. Nevertheless, Mr. Bruce and his several volumes give a very credible account to the historic Ethiopia of the period; although it was received by those who perused avidly and read his journals as a quite fantastic, unimaginable and even, to some – incredible fable in his native Protestant England at the time. It would be a while before others would follow his footsteps attempting to verify his report. We are persuaded that it was here that the definition of Negro and Ethiopian, or pseudonymously "Abyssinian" became attached to one another to refer to most 'Black' people, at home and abroad.

IN SUMMARY, therefore, the First and the New Haile Selassie I Bible both must be rightfully regarded and accepted as both indigenous and authentic Judeo-Christian contributions to the community of Ethiopian-Hebrews, at home and abroad, and also to the Rastafari faithful; with due regard and emphasis paid to the Ethiopian monk named Abu Rumi and 'His' translation that, at best, due to outside influences and intents, quite imperfectly proceeded it, due more to the influence of the European missionaries, mainly the British Bible Societies whose intention appears genuine but nevertheless foreign and subject to certain doubts that have been addressed in this brief treatment on the matter. Nevertheless, the Abu Rumi translation should not be confused with the Emperor's first or revised version that represent a uniquely Ethiopian and Imperial achievement based upon Ethiopic MSS and not a translation of a translation, as was the case in part with the Abu Rumi text.

The latter day, post-Haile Selassie Amharic Bible translations, namely the UBS Versions (1987, 2005) and the IBS Version (2001) are nothing more, from a point of linguistic authenticity, English-based translations into a modern form of Colloquial Amharic, whose only seeming advantage is being easy-to-read, but poor theologically and flawed severely at many points of departure for the True Faith of Ethiopia. These last two Versions, the UBS and the IBS Amharic Bibles are, in our scholarly opinion based upon diligent examination of all versions cited here, simply Mystery Babylon's or Western [Euro & Anglo-American] *pseudo*-Christianity's latest version of covert spiritual warfare against the unassuming and careless Ethiopian Amharic-speaking Christian. It is a shame that many Ethiopians know what we are saying to be the truth but have remained silent to these spiritual attack against the Ethiopian faithful who have been given a stone instead of a loaf of bread, a serpent instead of a fish – because of the slander and blasphemy against His Imperial Majesty and His Authorized Amharic Bible, the "Book of the Seven Seals."

One must recall that when the First Haile Selassie I Bible (1935) was still in the press when the Anti-Christ papal fascist armies lead by Benito Mussolini invaded Holy Ethiopia. Was this just a coincidence? Or, was it just another prophetic 'sign of the time' concerning "Christ in His Kingly character"?

Because the enemies of the 'rise of the [Black] Messiah,' who is "Christ in His Kingly character," were unable to stop His Imperial Majesty or the prophetic publication of His "Amharic Bible," the 'Book of the Seven Seals' they instead had opted to produce counterfeit

Amharic-based versions of the Bible that were only Amharic translations of formerly existing European editions used by the Anglo missionaries based up very questionable versions of English language "New World" and "Good News" so-called Bibles, most recently published in the Western Christians. One only need to review the controversy concerning the "Good News," NIV, NASV and other such 'New Translations' in modern English to witness the lack of authenticity and theological discrepancies that have been discovered in them to know more about why these bibles should not be trusted or regarded with any acceptance as anything respecting the 'Word of God.' The divinity of Christ has been put into doubt and removed from several places in the newer English and English-to-Amharic Bible, like the UBS and the IBS.

These subjects, very important as a background to the bible version controversy, have been addressed by other authors, scholars and bibliolators; therefore we find it unnecessary at this point to regurgitate the details that are known and available to the reader elsewhere.

Of the Five (5) that we have briefly referred to, the 2nd and 3rd, namely the First and the New Haile Selassie I Bible, published or known internationally in 1935 and 1962 respectively are the best versions of the Amharic, when compared diligently to the ancient Hebrew, Greek (LXX) and the Ethiopic (Ge'ez); they remain consistent and in some instances even superior to the known and received versions based upon a variety of criteria established by the Biblical Scholarship; however, the order should be reversed in merit of best to worst, i.e. New Haile Selassie I Bible, First Haile Selassie I Bible, Abu Rumi translation, and the UBS and IBS are equally bad English-to-Amharic copies used by the foreign and 'Pente' missionaries to Ethiopia and careless Ethiopians in the diaspora.

Amharic Translations of the Bible (Our New Ordering from Better Version to Worst Versions)

- **1 New Haile Selassie I Bible (1962)**
- **2 First Haile Selassie I Bible (1935)**
- **3 Abu Rumi translation (1860s?)**
- **4 UBS Versions (1987, 2005)**
- **5 IBS Version (2001)**

As we have demonstrated, there needs to be a reordering of the priority, quality, accuracy and authenticity of the version of the Amharic Bible beginning with the Emperor's Authorized, or *Revised Amharic Bible* of 1961/62 A.D. being the better, if not the best, as we have only begun to prove with these notes contained here. On the other hand, the so-called UBS to the IBS being, in our estimation, not even truly worthy of being classed similarly, yet only due to the subject matter discussed here do we include all the versions that have been published to date and available, in one form or another.

Thus, the former listing is only a linear timeline for the purposes of the student and reader to document what came when and before, or after which. It is simply a chronology, as it were, of the order of publication and not heirarchical or scientific in any sense. It is only for reference and comparison; a more throughout manuscript with samples and selections from each will be placed side-by-side and critically analyzed is forthcoming by this Author, one of the first to reveal the 'Book of the Seven Seals' (no. 3 on the list below, or the New Haile Selassie I Bible [1962[30]]).

History of Translations of the Bible into Amharic

- 1 Abu Rumi translation (1860s?)
- 2 First Haile Selassie I Bible (1935)
- 3 New Haile Selassie I Bible (1962)
- 4 UBS Versions (1987, 2005)
- 5 IBS Version (2001)

Until such time as a better and detailed critique can be presented to the reader, we have begun, in this the 50th year, or the "Jubilee Year," of the First Publication of the Emperor's Amharic Bible, originally on the 23rd of July, 1961, to reprint, in a series of Parallel Bible Versions (or, PBV) featuring both the Haile Selassie I Amharic Bible version side-by-side with the King James

---

[30] A double "Jubilee" is to be celebrated for the H.I.M. Haile Selassie I Bible because of the two dates that it was originally made available to both the Ethiopian indigenous Judeo-Christian community in 1961, on July 23rd, the Emperor's Birthday; and a year later – through the agreement originally made with the United Bible Society, this same UBS in 1962 AD, and thereafter published and disseminated to the world. Later, the UBS would discontinue the practice of distribution of the Authorized Amharic Bible and substitute it with an English-to-Amharic counterfeit that denies the Divinity of Christ, or the NIV and 'Good News Bible' licensed by the Vatican dissemblers of the True Faith.

Version, providing a Plain Text as the first, and in due time to be followed up by a Commentary[31] to each scroll or 'book' covered in the PBV series.

Through such PBV or Parallel Bible, namely RAB[32] and the KJV, we will have a better opportunity to compare and contrast two of the best versions of the Bible outside of the original and ancient versions, that are thought to be lost to antiquity, but recoverable in the Ethiopic and Emperor's *Amharic Bible*.

In closing this dissertation, we will include His Majesty's Preface to the Revised Amharic Bible and the English translation thereof as an ideal summary for all that we have attempted to communicate, disclose and document concerning the Haile Selassie I Bible, being the 'Book of the Seven Seals.' His Majesty's words express, directly and with authority both the genesis and the revelation of this, Our Holy Bible – the Revised Amharic Bible, who First Jubilee has come on what we know as the King's Sabbath, or 23rd July 2011 A.D.; the Second Jubilee will be in the 2012 on the same date, not a 'Sabbath,' but

---

[31] Or, as in the case of the recently published Amharic Psalms of David PBV a revision, annotation, commentary version, with transliterations where possible, that will assist the student and disciple in the diligent comparisons of the Authorized H.I.M. Amharic and the KJV English manuscript texts; both which celebrate, respectively their 50th (1st Jubilee) and 400th anniversary in the Anno Domini year 2011.

[32] This acronym stands for the *"Revised Amharic Bible,"* i.e. the Authorized 1961/62 AD version of the Amharic Bible originally published by the 'Lion of the Tribe of Judah' (Rev. 5:5): H.I.M. Haile Selassie I.

significant in other ways, both prophetic and earthshaking, to say the least. Some believe that the year 2012, according to the ancient Mayan astronomers and astrologers signifies the end of an Age and a time of galactic and cosmic alignment. Whether this is true is not a matter that we are able to discuss now in any detail, but – suffice it to say – the year 2012 has great significance to us in its own prophetic and relevatory way that should receive acceptance by all the sons and daughters of the King of Kings in Christ in His Kingly Character.

The following page features a sample transliteration of the very first Psalm of David from the Amharic Psalter of His Majesty. It serves as both a sample and a practice for those who are desirous of learning the Biblical Amharic of the H.I.M. Bible. The fidel, or syllabary and the Nibab Bet, or House of Reading are essential prerequisites to the 'loosening' and 'únsealing' of the seven seals, or seven tones or orders thereof.

Companion readers, guides and other study materials are currently in preparation, of which, a few have already been published and others are yet to be; these and more are expected to assist the new generation of Ethiopian-Hebrew students and Rastafari disciples of the Lion of Judah's order, the Society of His Majesty, with a greater comprehension and education in this discipline of study and exercise. The Society currently provides several initial Amharic Literacy materials and even digital media aids that are both free and easily affordable.

We depend on the Grace of the Almighty, and the faithful tithes, offerings and generousity of our brotherhood, members and Judeo-Christians of good will to continue and support this ministry of the Gospel of the King of Kings and His Christ. Therefore, we ask the reader to do all in their power, according to their faith and goodwill, to help disseminate and distribute these 'Teachings of His Majesty,' first to the Household of the Faith, i.e. Rastafari and the Ethiopian-Hebrew community, at home and abroad; and then to all those throughout the world who will receive our testimony to the Truth of the Revelation of God in Christ. May the Almighty bless you and keep you; and may the light and illumination of His countenance continue to shine upon all of you. AMEN AND AMEN.

33

THE 'BOOK OF THE GLORY OF KINGS' (KEBRA NAGAST) A WORK WHICH IS ALIKE THE TRADITIONAL HISTORY OF THE ESTABLISHMENT OF THE RELIGION OF THE HEBREWS IN ETHIOPIA, AND THE PATENT OF SOVEREIGNTY WHICH IS NOW UNIVERSALLY ACCEPTED IN ABYSSINIA AS THE SYMBOL OF THE DIVINE AUTHORITY TO RULE WHICH THE KINGS OF THE SOLOMONIC LINE CLAIMED TO HAVE RECEIVED THROUGH THEIR DESCENT FROM THE HOUSE OF DAVID.[34]

---

[33] This image represents the official logo of 'Ethiopia's Holy Bible Society,' founded by H.I.M. Haile Selassie I; in the Amharic it is known as *Ye'ItyoP'ya meS'haf q'dus mah'ber*, or – የኢትዮጵያ መጽሐፍ ቅዱስ ማኅበር.

[34] Taken from the colophon, the 'title page' of the English translation of the Kebra Nagast, renamed – "The Queen of Sheba & Her only son Menyelek," translated by Sir. Wallis E.A. Budge; 1922.

The Appendix
&
Selected Endnotes

Princes shall come out of Egypt; Ethiopia shall soon stretch out her hands to God.

መኳንንት ከግብጽ ይመጣሉ ኢትዮጵያ እጆችዋን ወደ እግዚአብሔር ትዘረጋለች።

THE PSALMS OF DAVID 68, VERSE 31

ሞዓ፡ አንበሳ፡ ዘእምነገደ፡ ይሁዳ፡
ቀዳማዊ፡ ኃይለ፡ ሥላሴ፡
ሥዩመ፡ እግዚአብሔር፡ ንጉሠ፡ ነገሥት፡ ዘኢትዮጵያ።

ORIGINAL: This work is in the public domain because it was first created in Ethiopia.

Under Title XI of the 1960 Ethiopian Civil Code, copyright exists only during the lifetime of the author.

In addition, any potential Ethiopian copyrights are non-binding in the United States, according to Circ. 38a of the US Copyright Office.

Translation by THE HAILE SELASSIE I PRESS, Ethiopia:

This work is in the public domain worldwide because it has been so released by the copyright holder.

መቅድም ፡

ምዓ ፡ አንበሳ ፡ ዘእምነገደ ፡ ይሁዳ ።
ቀዳማዊ ፡ ኃይለ ፡ ሥላሴ ፡
ሥዩመ ፡ እግዚአብሔር ፡ ንጉሠ ፡ ነገሥት ፡ ዘኢትዮጵያ ።

የክርስቲያን ፡ ደለት ፡ የሆነች ፡ ኢትዮጵያ ፡ አስቀ ድሞ ፡ ብሉይ ፡ ኪዳንን ፡ ቀጥሎም ፡ ሐዲስ ፡ ኪዳንን ፡ በመቀበል ፡ ከአብዛኞቹ ፡ አገሮች ፡ ቀዳሚነት ፡ ያላት ፡ መሆንዋን ፡ በታሪክ ፡ እንዲ ፡ ተመሰክሮ ፡ በመጣ ፡ ብሉይ ፡ ሕገ ፡ ኦሪትን ፡ በመጣ ፡ ሐዲስ ፡ ሕገ ፡ ወንጌልን ፡ በተቀበለች ፡ ጊዜ ፡ ቅዱሳት ፡ መጻሕፍት ፡ በጥንታዊ ፡ ጽንጾዋ ፡ በሕግ ፡ እንዲተረጐሙ ፡ አደረገች ። ከዚያም ፡ ወዲህ ፡ ለመንፈሳዊና ፡ ለሥጋዊ ፡ እውቀት ፡ ጠቃሚ ዎች ፡ የሆኑ ፡ አያሌ ፡ መጻሕፍት ፡ በየጊዜው ፡ የተደረሱትና ፡ የተጻፉት ፡ በግዕዝ ፡ ቋንቋ ፡ ነው ። ጊዜውና ፡ ዘሙኑ ፡ በሚቀደሙ ፡ መጠን ፡ በብዙ ፡ ትጋትና ፡ ድካም ፡ ሠርተው ፡ ለሃያማኖት ፡ መጠበቂያ ፡ ለትምህርትና ፡ ለእ ውቀት ፡ ማስፋፊያ ፡ የሚሆኑ ፡ መጻሕፍትን ፡ ላቁዩልን ፡ ለቀድሞዎች ፡ አበዎች ፡ ከፍ ፡ ያለ ፡ ምስጋና ፡ ይድረሳ ቸው ። እያለን ፡ እናስተውሳቸዋለን ።

በፈተችው ፡ ዘመናት ፡ ግዕዝ ፡ ያገረቱ ፡ ቋንቋ ፡ ስለ ነበረ ፡ ሕዝቡ ፡ ያለ ፡ አስተርጓሚ ፡ የመጻሕፍትን ፡ ምሥ ጢር ፡ ለመመርመርና ፡ ለማረዳት ፡ ችግር ፡ አልነበረ በትም ፡ ነገር ፡ ግን ፡ ዘመናት ፡ በመመነ ፡ ሲታደልኩ ፡ እንደሚና ፡ ሁሉ ፡ ቋንቋም ፡ በቋንቋ ፡ መታከስ ፡ ልማዱ ፡ ስለ ፡ ሆነ ፡ ከግዕዝ ፡ የተወለደ ፡ አማርኛ ፡ ቀስ ፡ በቀስ ፡ እያለ ፡ አድጎ ፡ ወዲያው ፡ የሕዝብ ፡ መነጋገሪያ ፡ ሆነና ፡ የግዕዝን ፡ ስፍራ ፡ ወሰደ ። በዚህም ፡ ጊዜ ፡ የግ ዕሁን ፡ ቋንቋ ፡ ምሁራን ፡ የሆኑት ፡ የቤተ ፡ ክርስቲ ያን ፡ ሰዎች ፡ እንጂ ፡ ተራው ፡ ሕዝብ ፡ በተላ ፡ የማ ያስተውለው ፡ ሆነ ። ከዚህም ፡ የተነሣ ፡ ሊቀውንቱ ፡ የግዕዝን ፡ ቃል ፡ በአማርኛ ፡ እየተረጐሙ ፡ በማስረዳት ፡ ሲሰብኩና ፡ ሲሠሩ ፡ ብዙ ፡ ዘመናት ፡ አለፉ ፡ ይኸውም ፡ ሁኔታ ፡ እስከ ፡ እኛ ፡ ዘመን ፡ ድረስ ፡ የነበረ ፡ ነው ።

በእግዚአብሔር ፡ ቸርነት ፡ ለኢትዮጵያ ፡ ዙፋን ፡ ከተመረጥን ፡ ጀምሮ ፡ ሕዝባችን ፡ በትምህርትና ፡ በእ ውቀት ፡ እንዲድግ ፡ ስንመራው ፡ በመንፈሳዊም ፡ በሥጋዊም ፡ ትምህርትና ፡ እንዲያድግ ፡ እስ በን ፡ በተቻለን ፡ ሁሉ ፡ ደከምንለት ፡ ወደዚህም ፡ ግብ ፡ ለመድረስ ፡ አስቀድሞ ፡ ቅዱሳት ፡ መጻሕፍትን ፡ በማርኛ ፡ ማስተርጐምና ፡ አብያቶ ፡ ማሳተም ፡ የሚያ ስፈልግ ፡ መሆኑን ፡ ስለተረዳን ፡ በ፲፱፻፳፮ ፡ ዓ. ም. ገና ፡ በአልጋ ፡ ወራሽነትና ፡ በእንደራሴነት ፡ ሳለን ፡ ከኢት ዮጵያ ፡ ሊቀውንት ፡ መካከል ፡ መርጠን ፡ መጻሕፍትን ፡ እንዲተረጐሙ ፡ አድርገን ፡ ንዕቡን ፡ ክነማደረውን ፡ በትርጓሜ ፡ አስወጣነት ፡ ቀጥሎም ፡ በግል ፡ ገንዘብ ፡ ተጥሚያ ፡ መኪና ፡ ከአውሮፓ ፡ አስመተናና ፡ ተተሚያ ፡ ቤት ፡ አቋቁመን ፡ መጻሕፍትን ፡ ማሳተም ፡

ጀምረን ። በዚያን ፡ ጊዜ ፡ በግዕዝና ፡ በአማርኛ ፡ ያለ ፡ ተምናቸው ፡ ጥቂቶቹ ፡ መጻሕፍት ፡ በአብያተ ፡ ክርስቲ ያናትና ፡ በየሕዝቡም ፡ ቤት ፡ እየተገዙም ፡ የሚዳማትን ፡ ማጽኛ ፡ የመፈረስ ፡ መበረታት ፡ ሆነው ፡ ተንኝቷል ። ከዚያም ፡ በኋላ ፡ የሕዝቡ ፡ አእምሮ ፡ በማስተ ፡ ዋል ፡ እየደረ ፡ መሔዱን ፡ ተመልክተን ፡ በኢትዮጵያ ፡ ቤት ፡ ክርስቲያን ፡ ሥርዓት ፡ ፰ቱ ፡ (፰ቱም) ፡ ተቢ ለው ፡ የሚቄጠሩት ፡ የብሉይና ፡ የሐዲስ ፡ ኪዳን ፡ መጻ ሕፍት ፡ በንጠላ ፡ ዘይቤ ፡ በአማርኛ ፡ እንዲተረጐሙ ፡ አደረግን ። ሊቃውንቶቻችንም ፡ ትርጉሙን ፡ ፈጽ መው ፡ በ፲፱፻፶፫ ፡ ዓ. ም. ስላቀረቡልን ፡ እንዲታተም ፡ አዝዘን ፡ መጽሐፉ ፡ በማተሚያ ፡ ቤት ፡ ሳለ ፡ ያዘዘቻቸው ፡ ዓ. ም የጠላት ፡ ወረራ ፡ የሥራው ፡ መጠናቀቅ ፡ ሆኖ ፡ ይሁን ፡ እንጂ ፡ በስይቱ ፡ ዘመን ፡ ስንፊን ፡ ላይ ፡ ሳለን ፡ ይኸው ፡ መጽሐፍ ፡ ቅዱስ ፡ በሮቻ ፡ አፍ ፡ ሌት ፡ እንዲ ታተም ፡ ስለ ፡ ፈቀድንና ፡ ታትም ፡ ስለ ፡ ወጣ ፡ የኢት ዮጵያ ፡ መመለስ ፡ በተስፋ ፡ እየተጠባበቁ ፡ በያሉ በት ፡ ይነቡት ፡ ኢትዮጵዋያን ፡ ዜጋዎቻችንን ፡ በዚህ ፡ መጽሐፍ ፡ ቅዱስ ፡ ሃይማኖታቸውን ፡ አየጠበቁ ፡ ሁሉን ፡ ወደሚቻል ፡ እምላክ ፡ ጸሎት ፡ ያቀርቡበት ፡ ነበር ።

ለእግዚአብሔር ፡ ክብር ፡ ምስጋና ፡ ይድረሰውና ፡ የኢትዮጵያን ፡ ነጻነት ፡ አስመልሰን ፡ ከንግሥተ ፡ ነገሥት ፡ መንግሥታችን ፡ ከገባን ፡ በኋላ ፡ የመጻሕፍ ፡ ቅዱስ ፡ ትርጉም ፡ ከመሠረታዊ ፡ ቋንቋው ፡ አስተራያ ስተና ፡ ከሶርዕ ፡ ጋር ፡ እየተያዘ ፡ ሊታረም ፡ እንዲማገባው ፡ ስለ ፡ ተመለከትን ፡ በቅዱሳት ፡ መጻሕፍት ፡ ትምህርት ፡ ለዚህ ፡ ሥራ ፡ ተገቢ ፡ የሆኑትን ፡ ሊቃውንት ፡ መርጠን ፡ በየካቲት ፡ ፳፯ ፡ ቀን ፡ ፲፱፻፴፱ ፡ ዓ. ም. እንድ ፡ የመጻ ሕፍ ፡ ቅዱስ ፡ ኮሚቴ ፡ በቤተ ፡ መንግሥታችን ፡ ግቢ ፡ እንዲቋቋም ፡ አደረግን ፡ ኮሚቴውም ፡ ፯ ፡ ዓመት ፡ ያህል ፡ በትጋትና ፡ በቅንነት ፡ ሠርቶ ፡ በሚያዝያ ፡ ፲፰ ፡ ቀን ፡ ፲፱፻፵፮ ፡ ዓ. ም. አቀረበልን ። በዚህ ፡ ሥራ ፡ ላይ ፡ ለረድናና ፡ ላገነዝሱ ፡ ሁሉ ፡ ከብ ፡ የሆነ ፡ ምስ ጋና ፡ እንሰጣቸዋለን ።

በመጽናትና ፡ መጻሕፍት ፡ በሚሰጡት ፡ መጽና ራት ፡ ተስፋ ፡ ይሆንልን ፡ ዘንድ ፡ የተጻፈው ፡ ሁሉ ፡ ለትምህርታችን ፡ ተጻርኋል ፡ ከመጻሕፍትም ፡ የሚጊ ንው ፡ ብርኃን ፡ ለሁሉ ፡ እንዲያበራ ፡ ስለ ፡ ተመኘን ፡ ይሀ ፡ መጽሐፍ ፡ ቅዱስ ፡ በኛ ፡ ትዝገነና ፡ ፈቃድ ፡ ታርሞና ፡ ተዚጋቅቶ ፡ በዘመነ ፡ መንግሥታችን ፡ በሀያ ፡ እምስትኛው ፡ ዓመት ፡ ታተመ ።

ሐምሌ ፡ ፳፪ ፡ ቀን ፡ ፲፱፻፵፱ ፡ ዓ. ም.
ቀዳማዊ ፡ ኃይለ ፡ ሥላሴ ፡ ን. ነ.

107

ENGLISH TRANSLATION

The following is the standard English translation of the *"meqdem"* or
"FOREWORD" that wasoriginally printed in the "Book of the
Seven Seals" (Revelation 5: 5) otherwise known as the 1961
AUTHORIZED H.I.M. HOLY BIBLE. Read, study and
meditate upon the Word of Truth revealed to us by
The Conquering Lion of The Tribe of Judah,
H.I.M. HAILE SELLASSIE I,
Elect of GOD,
King of Kings of Ethiopia.
Compare with: Rev. 5:5; Amos 9:7-11; Zech. 3:9-10.

The "REVISED AMHARIC BIBLE"

by Haile Selassie, translated by Haile Selassie I Press
Information about this edition: Speech of July 23, 1961

Ethiopia, an island of Christianity, is recorded in history as having received first the Old Testament, and then the New Testament earlier than most of the countries of the world. When, in Old Testament times, she received the Law, and when, in New Testament times, she received the Gospel, she ensured that the Scriptures were translated into the ancient language of GE'EZ. From those times to this, various books both of spiritual and material profit have periodically been compiled and written in GE'EZ. We remember with deep gratitude those fathers of old who, as time and opportunity allowed, worked with much care and labour and have left us books for the preservation of the Faith and for the increase of learning and knowledge.

In former ages, GE'EZ was the language of the country and so even without an interpreter, the people had no difficulty in examining and understanding the books; but just as one age succeeds another, so Amharic, Which sprang from GE'EZ, gradually grew until it became the Common speech of the people, taking the place of GE'EZ. At that time. GE'EZ was understood by the learned People of the Church; but was not readily understood by the ordinary people. Arising from this, the scholars in their preaching and work have for centuries been forced in their teaching to interpret from GE'EZ into Amharic. And these conditions prevailed until Our own times.

Since the time when, by God's goodness, We were chosen to ascend the Throne of Ethiopia and while We have been leading Our people to progress in learning and knowledge, We have laboured in every way possible with an eye to their growth in spiritual and material learning and knowledge. In. order to reach this goal, and realizing that the first necessity was to have the Scriptures translated into Amharic and printed in bulk, in 1918 when We were still Heir to the Throne and Regent, We chose from amongst the scholars some to translate the Scriptures and to produce the translation alongside the GE'EZ. After this, too, at Our private expense We had a printing machine brought from Europe, established a Printing Press, and began to have books printed. Some of the books which We caused to be printed in GE'EZ and Amharic at that time, read in churches and homes, have been found profitable to the establishment of faith and to spiritual strengthening. After that, noting that the mind of the people continued to grow in understanding, We arranged for a word-for-word translation into Amharic of the books of the Old and New Testaments. Our scholars completed the translation and presented it to Us in 1931, and We ordered its printing. While the book was still in the Press, however, enemy aggression in 1935 halted the work. Even so, when in exile in London, We gave permission for this same Bible to be printed by photo-offset, and it was duly issued. By this Book, Our Ethiopian subjects in exile in many countries held fast to their faith and presented their petitions to

Almighty God as they awaited the restoration of Ethiopia.

When, all honour and praise be to God, We had brought about the liberation of Ethiopia and had entered Our Empire, realizing that there ought to be a revision from the original Hebrew and Greek of the existing translation of the Bible, We chose scholars qualified for the work of Biblical training and on March 6th, 1947 set up a Bible Committee in Our Palace. The Committee worked with diligence for some five years, and on April 19th. 1952 presented the translation to Us. We give heartfelt thanks to all who helped Us in this work. All the ancient Scriptures were written for Our instruction, in order that through the encouragement they give Us, we may maintain Our hope with fortitude. Because We desire that the light which comes from the Scriptures may shine to all, this Bible by Our command and will has been revised and printed in the Thirty-First year of Our reign.

THE LION OF JUDAH HATH PREVAILED,

H.I.M. HAILE SELASSIE I,

Elect of GOD,

King of kings of Ethiopia

Said To Be His Imperial Majesty's Favorite Picture

c. 1930 A.D.

Isaiah Chapter 63, Verse 1

"Who is this that cometh from Edom, with dyed garments from Bozrah? this that is glorious in His apparel, travelling in the greatness of His strength? I, that speak in Righteousness, mighty to save."

More Preliminary Notes on the 'Book of the Seven Seals' & the Relationship to the Queen of the South, i.e. the Ethiopian Queen of Sheba.

In drafting, composing and compiling the proofs, texts and references for this volume on the Haile Selassie I Revised Amharic Bible, that we had identified and assert is the prophetic "Book of the Seven Seals," mentioned in the Revelation of St. John, a very interesting correspondence and comparison, that we would like to share; again became increasing clear, apparent and plainly evident to us. In the Gospels, the Saviour proclaims and makes a correlation between the ንግሥተ ዓዜብ[35] "Queen of the South" and the end-time judgment of the "times of the Gentiles."[36] Now the "Queen of the South" is also known and sometimes referred to as the "Queen of Sheba." The KAMO-SEMITIC[37] word and name, "Sheba"

---

[35] This phrase ንግሥተ ዓዜብ is found in both St. Matthew 12:42 and St. Luke 11:31; however the Ethiopic [Archaic Amharic] word for "South" or ዓዜብ in the first instance is ዓዜብ 'Azeb ['Azêb; 'Azeyb] using the ዓ Ayn (ayin) "A" ('), the so-called Asperin sonant, while on the other hand, in the second citation we find ንግሥተ አዜብ from the latter Synoptic Gospel of St. Luke. Here, the same two-part word is rendered with the 'Alef [Aleph] "A" (') reflecting *spiritus lenis*; the linguistic differences clearly between the Hebrew 'Matthew' and the Greek 'Luke' where both sounds, due to the limitation of the Greek language, are rendered, sadly, one and the same. Another note is that the Amharic word for 'north' ሰሜን Semên was, in older Ethiopic, used to point to the 'southern' direction in ancient times; to his noteworthy credit, the self-taught Egyptologist Gerald Massey is one of the first, if not only, writers to grasp and explain this mystery that resolves much on-going controversies of the past.

[36] St. Luke 21:24; or, "አሕዛብ ዘመን"

[37] See my late father, Rafiyq Ahmed Abdul-Hamiyd's groundbreaking dissertation published in Muhammad Speaks, March 6th 1970 article, History of Black Civilization, and the recently fully published 4-part overview study entitled – *The Antiquities of the Black Race*, printed by Lion of Judah Society Publishers.

113

derived from the more ancient "Seba" means simply 'seven' in relation to the primordial seven (7), and also applied in the bible to the "sacred oath" and the inherent idea of "covenant." In its simplest aspect, the SHEBA and SEBA relates to "SEVEN" and can also be expanded to point to, and/or include the idea of "The SEVENTY[38]." *Mathematically*, using the *Arabo-European* numbers, this would be accomplished by a mere addition of a "zero" or a cipher to the base number − 7, or − 7 + 0 = 70. Now, as easy as this may be done in numbers and counting, if we "do the math," in a linguistic and root etymological way, the very same is also true in the application of the science, or *scientia*[39] − "knowledge". Thus, why and how is this important in our discussion of the "Book of the Seven Seals"?

Firstly, it is the name, or "Shem" (ስም S'M [Sım] − for 'name; nomos' and ሴም SÊM — for the Hebraic 'SHEM') that provides the initial clues and if followed carefully and diligently, the answer is embedded in itself, such as fractals

---

[38] In Greek "seventy" is known as "Septuagint" or Romanized as "LXX" provides the key link between the first non-Hebrew Holy Bible translation; there are unsubstantiated tales spread to its origins, however, there is clear indications to speculate that the so-called Septuagint Bible was originally formed from a Sabaean version from the Queen of Sheba period that was later translated into Coptic and afterwards was rendered into Greek by so-called Hellenized [Black] Hebrews, or early Ethiopian 'Jews' in the Mediterranean areas and the Egypts. The connection between the Sabaean identity and the Roman 3rd century rape of the Sabines must also be considered and explored further.

[39] This word being of Latin is equivalent to the Greek γνοσισ (gnosis); the equivalent in the ancient Ethiopic [Ge'ez] and royal [Shoan] Amharic of the Haile Selassie I Bible is the same, usually − አእምሮ Aemmro [እ፰ሙር Aymero], interpretively, referential to the mind.

repeat the elemental fragment creating a self-reference. Nature itself, whether in the ancient "divinized" aspects reflective in the forms and formations based upon the abstract [mythological] or spiritual unseen, but knowable in heart [consciousness] and the mind. The *Sheba* and *Seba* correspondence is thus evident in the fact that, in the Amharic language, the word for "seven" is ሰባት Sebat. The final terminative "-t" (-ት) is a feminizing suffix that gives to any word that it is attached to a specific and an intimate relation, unlike the general form, which is male, and this lends to the opposite being true. In the Ethiopic and old Ge'ez, the word for "seven" is ሰብዕ Seb'I or simplified as ሰብ Seb', the ancient word for "Man," literally to *incarnate*. Even the Ethiopic cipher or number is interesting and may be studied and compared separately as to relevance with and in the context of the present discussion. The Ethiopic cipher[40], or አኻዝ AKHAZ [or, Ahaz] is endered as follows (፯).

Another way that the verse or phrase in Revelation Chapter 5, namely verse 5 can be translated instead of as "the Book of the Seven Seals" could be "the Book of the *Sheba* Seals." What would these "Sheba Seals" or SABAEAN "seals" be? Whatever they would be, they definitely must be related to "the Queen of the South," i.e. the "Queen of Sheba" and therefore "Ethiopia and the Bible." Any doubt about that

---

[40] Also may be rendered in common Amharic as ቁጥር *q'uT'r*, or number.

would be religiously irrelevant, spiritually fraudulent and intellectually very dishonest because to deny that would be to deny the very context of both the scriptures and the true "history" of the faithful ancients as testified to both by Hebrew testimony and the Egyptian records. But, this is what may have done – deny the context and then interpolate conclusions that could never be germane to the subject when based upon facts and the key factors of the KAMITE Mythology, the framework of the biblical matter.

If Sheba is interpreted correctly to mean and refer to the "seven," does the idea of "South" also imply the same? What could be the coincidence of the matter that the "Queen of Sheba," who is identified accurately as the "Queen of the South," are both located in the "Ethiopic" regions, particularly the highland and source of the waters of the Nile; produces and gives birth to the only potentate in his time, the "King of Kings[41]" and a ancient Hebraic culture, that is definitely biblical by divine design, also producing an ancient scriptural evidence and literature that testifies to Her own Divine Heritage and covenant status as a bride; if not, in fact and reality, *the* bride of the Christ [i.e. the Anointed] King? Could all of this be the merest coincidence and a simple matter of vain human effort based upon luck devoid of any divine providence, no doubt, guiding *gradually* all these events and circumstances? We cannot and

---

[41] See 1st Timothy 6:15, which reads: "Which in his times he shall shew, who is the blessed and only Potentate, *the King of kings*, and Lord of lords"

will not attempt to be dishonest and disingenuous, like some careless Ethiopians and others, and in vain controvert the plain truth that is so easily and readily demonstrated in a multitude of self-referential ways.

We must conclude then that when we examine the SHEMITIC sense of "Sheba" and compare it with the KAMITE Mythos, in light of the Revelation of St. John, fulfilling in the manifestation of the Ethiopian Emperor, HAILE SELASSIE I – it is the one too many of the 'incidents' that go far beyond mere co-incidence. Even more so than this, we should not forget that the well-known and aptly ascribed Psalm 68, verse 31 that testifies to "PRINCES SHALL COME OUT OF EGYPT, ETHIOPIA SHALL STRETCH FORTH HER HANDS TO GOD" also provides, as it were, a proverbial string for the pearls to be brought together as a priceless gem of rare stones, even the very "cornerstone" which in its Greek Septuagint LXX Version points again to "Egypt." In fact, the word for "head cornerstone" and "chief cornerstone" has been claimed to be, in the Greek, pyramidion or simply "pyramid." Unfortunately, this is not true. The facts, according to the true linguistics and etymology of the English word 'pyramid' comes from the Latin *pyramides*, the plural of *pyramis*, from the Greek *puramis*, whose roots is in the old Egyptian PI-MAR, or commonly *Pimar*.

The Greek word for 'capstone,' head cornerstone and chief cornerstone is *koruphôsis*. The word found in the Greek Bible for 'capstone' is mistranslated and should be first 'stone,' or beginning stone, i.e. the first laid at the start of a building project. The true biblical sense is foundation stone, or in Greek, *akrogôinaios*[42]. Theologically, Christ Jesus is the foundation, or first stone; likewise, based upon His own words, Ethiopia through the "Queen of the South" points and reveals the same. Therefore, at each step and in whatever direction that we turn, we find ancient and biblical matter of our subject to fit like a custom tailored, intricately designed and interwoven garment – of many colours. These colours are not mundane, but of heavenly hue, or 'blue' (sapphire?); in and of themselves reflect the primary pattern of the rainbow, the *very* sign given since the "days of Noah," if not, as some maintain, even previous thereto.

"As it was in the beginning, so shall it be in the end" is a faithful and worthy proverb and an hieroglyphic parable made abstract yet easily demonstrated as a cipher or circle in its simplest form and figure. *"The first shall be last, and the last shall be first"* also recasts the same abstract ore to produce, through refinement, an equal measure of gold and precious mental metals. The Hebrew Bible, the Christian Old Testament gives us a historicity of the ancient mythology when it begins, after the *"in the beginning"* of book one, chapter one. With the second chapter of Genesis, here is introduced, to our modern world's

---

[42] See Strong's Concordance G204 reference found in the New Testament Septuagint (LXX), the *Koine* Greek Bible version of Ephesians 2:20; 1ˢᵗ Peter 2:6 where Ακρογοιναιοσ, or "foundation stone" is found.

spiritual and cultural amnesiatic condition, *"the whole land of Ethiopia"* as it was and still is a known, evident and still existent "place" for the first-time origins in relation to the very first element mentioned, namely: the waters embodied by the "river." Need we remind the reader that "water is life" in the essential nature of human existence as the majority of our earthly bodies are mainly consistent of such water? Or, the fact that is medically proven – one may survive longer without food than without clean, drinking water? For those who are biblically and Christologically so inspired – BAPTISM is a sacred act that requires water as a main ingredient and even when interpreted more spiritual, in accordance with Christian maturation, the idea and thought of the "word," or λογοσ acting as "water" for washing and cleansing (of our conscience) is equally and metaphysically applicative, if not highly relevant[43].

It has become a sort of RASTAFARIAN proverb that *"in the abundance of water, the fool is still thirsty,"* so we ask: Is water, or wisdom, taken too often for granted? Squandered? Wasted? The poverty of the present Human condition is in the sad reality that money, or the inordinate love thereof, is so greatly valued that it has been forgotten that it was only a currency created by the Human condition for the human condition. Man thus

---

[43] Acts of the Apostles 11:16, or "Then remembered I the word of the Lord, how that he said, John indeed baptized with water; but ye shall be baptized with the Holy Spirit." Compare with Ephesians 5:25-26, in part: "That he might sanctify and cleanse it *with the washing of water by the word*,"

denies the signs of the living God and takes dead things made by himself as the currency or energy of his "life;" and to what end? It is to his death and the death of "his kind," – that is, mankind; of course, his own living death is just like the vain and dead things, or manufactures, that he and his kind has erroneously placed so much "worth-ship," or love upon and chooses to worship such instead of the very living God who created the living elements that he buys and sells?! Who is this "God," the One who created the living elements or the seven elemental planes of existence?

There can be no doubt or question to those initiated and illuminated by the light of the truth, in the living spirit of their own lives, that this "God" is and was known as the ELOHIM, or the TRIUNE GOD. And it is here again that we encounter "the seven," whether the "seven spirits" or the "seven elemental planes," from protoplast to the realm of the Cherubim, the "divine mathematics" still adds up and yield the same One. In this is another cipher completed, namely – *"Ethiopia stretching her hands to God [or, Elohim]."* ELOHIM is that "God" of the Seven and thus the true "God" and divinity of the primordial and ancient Sabaeans and blameless Ethiopians. So "Ethiopia" stretches her 'hands' [this is obvious a dual; or two hands] to the ELOHIM, the God of the Seven, the TRIUNE GOD and the SHEBA, i.e. the Oath and the Holy covenant could be said to be the *"conclusion of the whole matter."* But, of course, there is more – much more.

RAS IADONIS TAFARI

How I came to acquire My very First H.I.M. Amharic Bible, The Authorized 1961/62 A.D. Revised Amharic Version:

My first Amharic Bible, along with a companion Amharic-English Dictionary were given to me in early 1990/91 A.D., by my native-born Ethiopian tutor, Leah Tafari, to whom I am eternally grateful, in the name of God and Christ, for all her patience, diligence, assistance and the initial *fidel* instruction that was offered in kindness and love, without any material charge. Although she was a Tigrean-Ethiopian, she spoke quite fluent Amharic and was, at the time, herself a resident-student, I believe if I recall correctly, in a medical or related scientific discipline and in attendance at Hunter College, in New York City. I cannot now say what eventually became of her as we went our own ways, or her younger sister – not to mention her very young daughter, that no doubt, would herself be a grown and hopefully mature woman by this time. I pray that they are all well, healthy and prosperous in spirit and truth. Nevertheless, I think about her often when I remember the grace that I was shown and thus find it only appropriate and due to her openhandedness to make an opening mention and loving note of my dearest Sister Leah – she who showed me unadulterated kindness in my formative studies in the Amharic language and, above all, gave me the book – THE HAILE SELASSIE I BIBLE – *that* little book which would and did, *literally* change my life for the better and since then has become my favorite book *par excellence*.

I cannot adequately nor fully express my sincere appreciation enough for both Sister Leah Tafari and her generous gift; one that has greatly enabled me over the years to grow from a disciple to develop some degree of mastery in the "knowledge of the Son of God" as testified to and recorded in the pages of the Bible, and subsequently to gain an ever-growing proficiency in the both the archaic [biblical] and the modern Amharic, not to mention inspiration to become an autodidact in regards to the ancient Ethiopic [Ge'ez]. Without the earlier guidance and encouragement give by Sister Leah and many others, whose names have not been as memorable as *Woizero* Tafari, very little of this may have even been possible or likely to have occurred in quite the same way. As it is written, እግዚአብሔርገም ለሚወዱት እንደ አሳቡም ለተጠሩት ነገር ሁሉ ለበጎ እንዲደረግ እናውቃለን። *"And we know that all things work together for good to them that love God, to them who are the called according to his purpose."* ROMANS CHAPTER 8, VERSE 28

It is therefore important, timely and refreshing for me to testify and to give heartfelt thanks to as well as for those said people and significant persons who have touched my calling and whom I cannot attempt to repay other than these words that I now write and share with those interested readers who may be curious and desirous to know exactly how I came to be the revealer of His Majesty's Bible in the West to His namesakes, the Rastafarians and also one of the first of the proclaimers of the prophetic "Book of the Seven Seals," as it is written – Revelation of St. John Chapter 5, Verse 5.

ወደ ሮሜ ሰዎች 8

28 እግዚአብሔርንም ለሚወዱት እንደ አሳቡም ለተጠሩት ነገር ሁሉ ለበጎ እንዲደረግ እናውቃለን።

KJV

ROMANS, CHAPTER 8

28 And we know that all things work together for good to them that love God, to them who are the called according to his purpose.

There is a plethora of both internal and external evidences, correspondences and correlations that directly verifies and conclusively proves, beyond any doubt, that the H.I.M. Bible is indeed the prophecied, anticipated and actual "Book of the Seven Seals" of the fifth chapter of the Book of Revelation.

First of all, let us ask: What is a Seal? And, what is God' seal? A seal is something that has to do with legal affairs. A law is stamped with the official seal of the ruling or authorized government. A seal has three parts or aspects to it. These three are:

1. **The name of the ruler or sovereign.**
2. **The ruler or sovereign's title.**
3. **The territory or jurisdiction over which he rules or governs.**

Now, when the government seal is on a law, or on its currency, this, the "seal," or sign there of makes it official and the entire nation loyally stands behind it. In the case of God's seal, it makes His 'law' official and the whole universe, and all that is there in is submits loyally and likewise stands behind it. This is a general idea that best describes a seal, what it is and its applied usage, both with God and amongst man. It is said that anyone who is disloyal to the seal of the government, or its sovereign ruler, and to the law upon which it is attached, is regarded and looked upon as being disloyal or rebellious to the government and its sovereign itself.

In like manner, when a ruler of a government, say its king or Emperor's seal is placed in or upon His law to make it "official," and thus to ratify or justify it – the Almighty also has His seal in His law. In the scriptures, the Most High has said to His prophet: "Bind up the testimony, seal the law among my disciples." Isaiah Chapter 8, Verse 16. This verse is interesting in many ways, one of which is its mention and use of the word "disciples" in the Old Testament. This we will seek to expound on in a further essay devoted to that subject. But firstly, let us find out exactly how and more importantly, where we are sealed according to the aforementioned verse in Isaiah. The testimony is to be bound and the law is to sealed amongst God's true disciples, but where? The correct answer is that the "disciples" are sealed in the forehead or the frontal lobe that is also known as the "mind's eye" – the so-called 'third eye.' Christ also says and instructs His own disciples, then and now to "Let your eyes be single." The testimony and the law are to be in our heart, that is to say, our mind. In the New Covenant called the "New Testament," His promise to us is: "**15** Whereof the Holy Ghost also is a witness to us: for after that he had said before, **16** This is the covenant that I will make with them after those days, saith the Lord, I will put my laws into their hearts, and in their minds will I write them;" The Epistle to the Hebrews Chapter 10, Verse 15 – 16.

When we choose God's way, the Holy Spirit places the seal of God in our forehead, signifying that it is in our heart and mind. The forehead contains the "frontal lobe," the very section of the human brain where our conscience resides and dwells. When one receives the "seal" of the Almighty God in one's forehead, it means that you have it in your heart, mind and conscience. You have faith in it and you seek to be loyal to it.

In the same way that a government, say a kingdom and its ruler, whether king, emperor or sovereign uses its "seal" to enforce the laws of the nation, empire or territorial land, the Most High God uses His own "seal" likewise. In fact, humanity has learned these things from God and not vice-versa. Even the anti-christs or major tool of the "beast" attempts to use its seal, or "the mark of the beast," by contrast – to try to enforce his 'law [of sin]' instead or, or 'ánti' – in opposition to the True law of the Almighty and His Messiah. Compare with the Psalms of David 2:1-3.

The question for us here and now is: Where will we find the "seal of God" with its three corresponding parts or aspects? The true and faithful answer is at the very center, or the "heart" of His Pure law, i.e. often called the Ten Commandments (but better, 'the 10 words,' or *Decalogue*). Now, let us take a closer look at this for ourselves:

8 Remember the Sabbath day, to keep it holy.
የሰንበትን ቀን ትቀድሰው ዘንድ አስብ።

9 Six days shalt thou labour, and do all thy work:
ስድስት ቀን ሥራ ተግባርህንም ሁሉ አድርግ

10 But the seventh day is the sabbath of the Lord thy God: in it thou shalt not do any work, thou, nor thy son, nor thy daughter, thy manservant, nor thy maidservant, nor thy cattle, nor thy stranger that is within thy gates:
ሰባተኛው ቀን ግን ለእግዚአብሔር ለአምላክህ ሰንበት ነው አንተ፤ ወንድ ልጅህም፣ ሴት ልጅህም፤ ሎሌህም፣ ገረድህም፣ ከብትህም፤ በደጆችህም ውስጥ ያለ እንግዳ በእርሱ ምንም ሥራ አትሥሩ

11 For in six days the Lord made heaven and earth, the sea, and all that in them is, and rested the seventh day: wherefore the Lord blessed the Sabbath day, and hallowed it.
እግዚአብሔር በስድስት ቀን ሰማይንና ምድርን፤ ባሕርንም፤ ያለባቸውንም ሁሉ ፈጥሮ በሰባተኛው ቀን ዐርፏልና ስለዚህ እግዚአብሔር የሰንበትን ቀን ባርኮታል ቀድሶታልም።

– ኦሪት ዘጸአት EXODUS CHAPTER 20, VERSE 8-11

In the "heart" of the Ten Commandments is one of the first and only places in the Holy Bible that one may find "God's Seal." Next, let us examine the three parts or aspects of a seal that we have already outlined in regards to the "seal" of the Almighty.

1. His Name – the *"Lord,"* or YHWH
2. His Title – *"thy God,"* or ÊLÔHÊ-KÂ
3. His Territory – the *"heaven and earth, the sea, and all that in them is."*

This should not be considered as incredible, in fact, when understood in its own context it must be, and is, very credible because it is faithful and true. When we begin to comprehend this it will become overt and obvious to any one who is intellectually honest and endowed with a basic ability to use "know the truth" of the matter being discussed here will fully realize why Satan and his accomplices have, and continue to, work so vigorously hard to deceive humanity by hiding the truth of the importance of the Sabbath day and its sanctity or inherit 'holiness' from us in this, or 'his' present *world*, or *system of things*.

The *ever* Coming, or Revelation of "Christ in His Kingly character" has caused the phenomenon, the feared 'rise of the [Black] Messiah' initiating a change; from the Old World Order of "White Supremacy," or the Gentile World Domination called the 'Times of the Gentiles' to a New World and a New Age, or *Addis Zemen*…

MATTHEW CHAPTER 12, VERSE 42

ንግሥተ ዓዜብ በፍርድ ቀን ከዚህ ትውልድ ጋር ተነሥታ ትፈርድበታለች፤ የሰሎሞንን ጥበብ ለመስማት ከምድር ዳር መጥታለችና፤ እነሆም፥ ከሰሎሞን የሚበልጥ ከዚህ አለ።

"The queen of the south shall rise up in the judgment with this generation, and shall condemn it: for she came from the uttermost parts of the earth to hear the wisdom of Solomon; and, behold, a greater than Solomon is here."

PROVERBS CHAPTER 9, VERSE 1

ጥበብ ቤትዋን ሠራች፤ ሰባቱንም ምሰሶችዋን አቆመች።

"Wisdom hath builded her house, she hath hewn out her seven pillars:"

THE ORIGIN AND GROWTH OF THE ENGLISH BIBLE

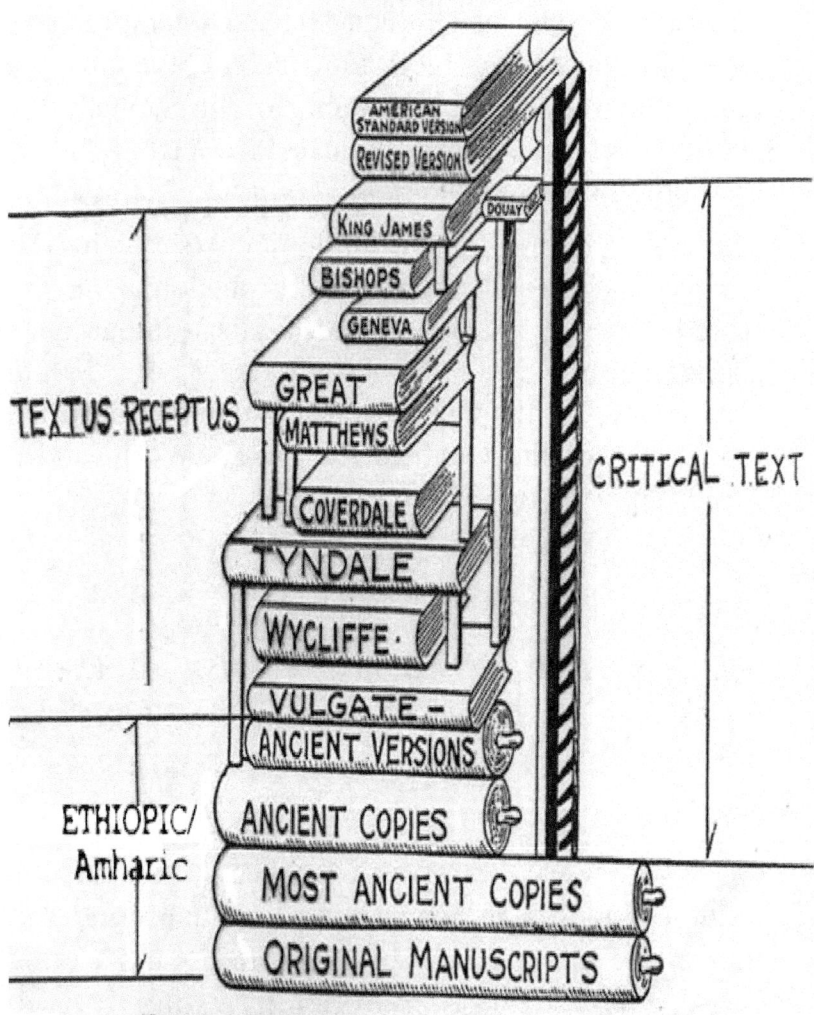

- AMERICAN STANDARD VERSION
- REVISED VERSION
- KING JAMES
- DOUAY
- BISHOPS
- GENEVA
- GREAT
- MATTHEWS
- COVERDALE
- TYNDALE
- WYCLIFFE
- VULGATE
- ANCIENT VERSIONS
- ANCIENT COPIES
- MOST ANCIENT COPIES
- ORIGINAL MANUSCRIPTS

TEXTUS RECEPTUS

CRITICAL TEXT

ETHIOPIC/Amharic

In the above drawing is shown the gradual development of the English Bible as well as the foundations upon which each successive version rests.

We are living in an age of printing.

It is hard for us to realize that when the books of the Bible were originally written, there was no printing press to multiply the copies.

Each copy must be made slowly and laboriously by hand. Under these conditions it was inevitable that many ancient books should be lost. This largely accounts for the fact that all the original manuscripts of the Bible have perished.

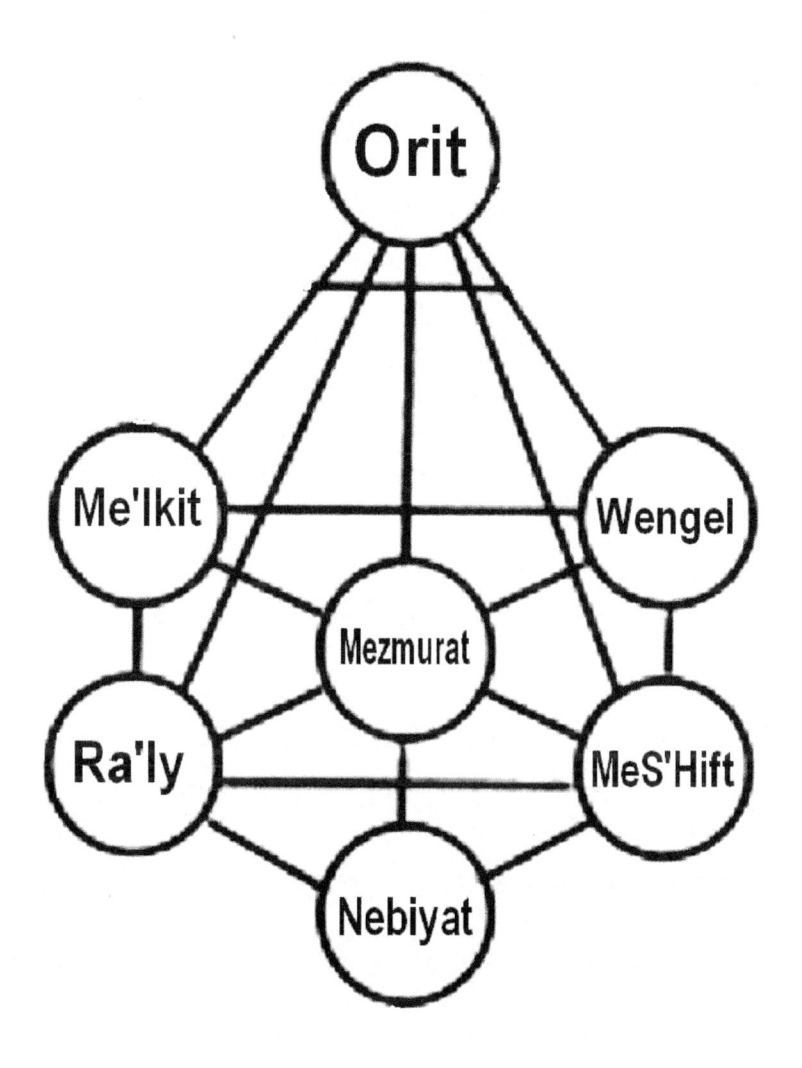

An Amharic Kabalistic (Cabbalistic) Tree of Life; H.I.M. Bible[44]

What are the **Seven Seals** of the Sacred Text found in the H.I.M. Holy Bible [Revised Amharic Bible]?

---

[44] Taken from the unpublished draft notes to the 'Amharic Kabbalah,' a study of the Book of the Seven Seals & Ethiopian-Hebrew mysticism of the His Majesty's Rastafari *Tewahedo* Church composed by the present author; above is pictured the Ethiopic *'tree of life'* based upon the 7 Seals of the H.I.M. Bible.

129

THE FIRST FOUR (4) SEALS ARE:

1. The OREET – the Ethiopian-Hebrew Torah
2. The MES'AH'FT – the Writings/Historical
3. The MEZAMURIT – the Psalms, Lamentations & Song of Songs of Selomon
4. The TINABEET – the Prophetical/ Nebiyat

There are FOUR (4) SEALS in the OLD TESTAMENT/ OLD COVENANT.

THEN, IN THE NEW TESTAMENT OR NEW COVENANT THERE ARE THREE (3) SEALS.

AND, THESE THREE (3) SEALS ARE:

5. The WENGELAWIT – the Gospels or GOODNEWS
6. The MEL'IK'TOCH – the EPISTLES or DIDACTICS
7. YE-YOHANNIS RA'IY – the VISION of the GRACE of YAH.

AND, WHAT IS THE MEANING AND SIGNIFICANCE OF EACH SEAL? The word "seal" in Amharic is called the ማተም Mahtem and ማኅተም Makhtem and has the meaning and signification of both "a seal" and "a [printed] stamp." Hence the word *Mahtem/ Makh-tem* refers to a printed ፊደል *fidel*, a letter, or literally – a syllable-sonant – that is so set to type [typeset]. A seal is also, in the sense of a sign, a symbol of rulership and mark of authority, or authorization.

On the very back of the book that is also known and called the spine of the book there are seven (7) Ethiopic letters that spells the መጽሐፍ ቅዱስ "Book [of the] Holy." This corresponds to what is said in Revelation Chapter 5 concerning seven (7) seals, or "prints" in reference to the typeset or printer's "stamps." This is the first aspect of the Revelation of the 'Book of the Seven Seals.' The correspondences with the seven pillars of Wisdom, or the seven charkas; these energy centers are cleansed and opened in the regenerated, or Born-Again/Born from above Man.

መጽሐፍ ቅዱስ
1 2 3 4 5 6 7

Behold! Look & See…

These are the 'Seven Seals,' or stamps/printers marks on the back of the Book published by the 'Lion of the Tribe of Judah' in 1961 A.D.

REVELATION CHAPTER 5, VERSE 5

"And one of the elders saith unto me, Weep not: behold, the Lion of the tribe of Juda, the Root of David, hath prevailed to open the book, and to loose the seven seals thereof."

The True GOOD NEWS, or *Gospel* of His Majesty, i.e. ተዋሕዶ TEWAH'DO!

WENDIM YADON, aka H.H. RAS IADONIS TAFARI is the Revealer of the Light/Illumination of the True GOODNEWS of His Imperial Majesty: QEDAMAWI HAILE SELASSIE (I) and the "True Bible of the Rastafari", the 1961 AUTHORIZED H.I.M. HOLY BIBLE in the Royal Language of the King of Kings of ETHIOPIA, the Kinsman Redeemer and the True "King of (Redeemed) ISRAEL" to the diaspora in the West, the lost sheeple of the House of Israel and the Elect, the Rastafari brothers, sisters and mothers. In addition, he has revealed to the Rastafari and disorientated "Rastas" the true meaning of the name and the Order of His Imperial Majesty, the Appointment of MELKE-SEDEQ. He has been explaining, correcting and enlightening the True Witness of His Imperial Majesty and the *"half of the story that has never been told....* **'till now!"**

Our Brother, Wendim Yadon[45] explains, corrects and illuminates the 'Word of God' based upon the 'Book of the Seven Seals,' the H.I.M. Haile Sellassie I Amharic Bible. He has also expounded in great detail these Teachings of His Majesty in recorded compositions on several hundreds of audio tapes, CDs, VCDs and DVDs containing the 1080 degrees of the RASTAFARI REVELATION of the "Son of Man" and His *Christos*: YAHOSHUWA HA-MESHIH with much more coming out every 13 months of sunshine. He has also translated both the Ethiopic (G'Iz) and Royal Amharic/Hebrew scriptures such as the Orit (5 Books of Musey), MeS'aH'ft, Mezamurit (MezmureDawit, S'qoqawe'Erm'yas, MekhaliyeMekhaliy ZeSelomon), Tinabit/Nebiyat, Wengelawit. Mel'Ik't, YeYohannis Ra'Iy these SEVEN SEALS including Heynok (Enoch), Kufaley (Jubilees) and more. He teaches the Ten (10) Commandments, the H'gg (the Law), the Shr'At (Ordinances), the F'rd/F'tha (Judgements/Justice) based upon various Ancient Teachings of the AmEn, so-called Ancient tribes and their Religions, Traditions, Scriptures, Ceremonies, and even the so-called Extraterrestrials all based upon the Holy Bible.

Within these scrolls (audio, video and analog files) you too find the Tewah'do mysteries revealed of the Father, the Son and the Holy Spirit as One, or *Ahadu* – embedded, fused and unified.

Coming soon Our ministry hopes to have available, both online & off – many more useful materials, sample texts and examples from many of the *Amharic* scrolls/books found in the H.I.M. Holy Bible and the Ethiopic ancient sacred scrolls. Please visit us online at: www.lojsociety.org and bookmark our site and all related companion and mirror sites on our network.

---

[45] This is Ras Iadonis' ETHIOPIAN BROTHERHOOD OF THE NAZARENE Hebraic '*shem*,' or name [s'm; sim in *Amharic*] and a proper communal appellation used amongst the Discipleship of the Household of the Faith, i.e. the Church of Rastafari and other mansions, branch or sister-societies of the LOJS. Thus saying *Wendim Yadon,* may be understood as translatable to 'Brother,' expressed by the Amharic *wendim* preceding the name – Yadon; that is, the Hebraic form of 'Iadonis' [or, Ιαδονοσ, Yadonos]. The royal protocol of the title-name 'Ras' expresses the reservation of usage amongst the true Rases when gathering together churchically; symbolic of the removing all crowns (titles) in the tabernacle or church for the Christ's sake, i.e. እናንተም ሁላችሁ ወንድማማች ናችሁ። "and all ye are brethren" (Matt. 23:8).

በዓይናችሁ ፊት ኢየሱስ ክርስቶስ እንደ ተሰቀለ ሆኖ ተሥሎ ነበር፤
"...before whose eyes JESUS CHRIST hath been evidently set forth, crucified..." – GALATIANS CHAPTER 3, VERSE 1

Our Ethiopian-Hebrew "JESUS CHRIST OF NAZARETH," ALONG WITH HIS DISCIPLES, MAGDALENE AND HIS MOTHER MARYAM.

A Transliteration of the H.I.M. Haile Selassie I Bible (Amharic): Psalm of David (or, the Mezmure Dawit) 'Chapter' or Psalm 1

1 ምስጉን ነው በክፉዎች ምክር ያልሄደ፤ በኃጢአተኞችም መንገድ ያልቆመ፤ በዋዘኞችም ወንበር ያልተቀመጠ።

2 ነገር ግን በእግዚአብሔር ሕግ ደስ ይለዋል፤ ሕጉንም በቀንና በሌሊት ያሰባል።

3 እርሱም በውኃ ፈሳሾች ዳር እንደ ተተከለች፤ ፍሬዋን በየጊዜዋ እንደምትሰጥ፤ ቅጠልዋም እንደማይረግፍ ዛፍ ይሆናል፤ የሚሠራውም ሁሉ ይከናወንለታል።

4 ክፉዎች እንዲህ አይደሉም፤ ነገር ግን ነፋስ ጠርጎ እንደሚወስደው ትቢያ ናቸው።

5 ስለዚህ ክፉዎች በፍርድ፤ ኃጢአተኞችም በጻድቃን ማኅበር አይቆሙም።

6 እግዚአብሔር የጻድቃንን መንገድ ያውቃልና፤ የክፉዎች መንገድ ግን ትጠፋለች።

1 msgun new bekfuwoch mkr yalhEde; bekhaTiÁtenyoch menged yalqome; bewazenyochm wenber yalteqemeTe:

2 neger gn be'saIgzi'AbHEr Hig dess yilewal; Higunm beqenna belElit yasbal:

3 Irsum bewkha fesashoch dar Inde tetekelech; frEwan beyeqizEwa IndemtseT; qTelwam Indemayregf zaf yhonal: yemisherawm hulu ykenawenletal:

4 kfuwoch Indih Aydelum; neger gn nefas Tergo Indemiwesdew tbiya nachew:

5 slezih kfuwoch befrd; khaTi'Atenyochim beSadqan makhber ayqomum:

6 Igzi'AbHEr yeSadqann menged yawqalna; yekfuwoch menged gn tTefalech:

His Imperial Majesty Haile Selassie I
Emperor of Ethiopia

ምስጉን ነው

WHO IS ABBA KEDDUS?[46]

አባ ቅዱስ
"Abba Keddus"

The Lion of "Judah"; Yoda of the Ethiopian Christian Knights; The Ancient Nazarene Order of the BAHITAWIS & Debteras!

---

[46] The one known to the world as H.I.M. HAILE SELASSIE I, is now known as *Abba Qiddus* or *Abba Keddus,* according to the transliteration used; He is the Holy Father, or the God-Father, *Kristina-Abb* of our Rastafari Faithful and all Holy Ethiopians/Africans and Gentile called by His name. It is a fact that H.I.M. was politically crucified being known as the Father of Modern and progressive Africa, but the anti-Christ Satanists and other agents of Mystery Babylon have attempted to thwart and abort His true witness of IYESUS KRISTOS. One only need recall and remember the prophecy of John Chapter 16 and one of the very

THE LUTHERAN HOUR: THE 1968 "CHRISTMAS DAY" INTERVIEW OF H.I.M. HAILE SELASSIE I AS INTERVIEWED BY DR. OSWALD HOFFMAN

December 25, 1968

YOUR IMPERIAL MAJESTY, IT IS A GREAT HONOUR TO BE PERMITTED TO SPEAK WITH YOU TODAY AND ALSO TO HAVE YOU AS A GUEST ON THIS SPECIAL CHRISTMAS PROGRAMME WHICH WILL BE BROADCAST TO PEOPLE ALL OVER THE WORLD. QUESTION: YOUR IMPERIAL MAJESTY, WHAT IS IT THAT MAKES YOU WANT TO FOLLOW JESUS CHRIST?

H.I.M. HAILE SELASSIE I: When Jesus Christ was born from Virgin Mary, from that time on He lived an exemplary life, a life which men everywhere must emulate. This life and the faith which He has taught us assures us of salvation, assures us also of harmony and good life upon earth. Because of the exemplary character of the life of Jesus Christ it is necessary that all men do their maximum in their human efforts to see to it

---

last interviews given by the King of kings of Ethiopia with the Italian journalist named Oriana Fallaci (now deceased) wherein He (still living) said and declared the following testimony (in part):"...since our Lord the Creator has deemed, We might serve our people as a Father serves his Son."

that they approximate as much as they can the good example that has been set by HIM. It's quite true that there is no perfection in humanity. From time to time we make mistakes. We do commit sins, but even as we do that, deep in our hearts as Christians we know we have a chance of forgiveness from the Almighty. He taught us that all men are equal regardless of sex, their national origin and tribe. And He also taught us all who seek HIM shall find HIM. To live in this healthy life, a Christian life, is what makes me follow Jesus Christ.

DR. HOFFMAN: Your Imperial Majesty, what advice would you give a person who is considering the claims of Christ, perhaps for the first time?

H.I.M. HAILE SELASSIE I: I would tell a person who was considering the claim of Christ for the first time that it is necessary to have faith in the Almighty, that it is necessary to have love, and that it is necessary to conduct oneself in a manner that we have been taught to do in the Bible.

I would also advise him to seek the secular knowledge, for the more one knows the more he realises the need for a prime mover, the need for a Creator, a Creator who is good, and the need for salvation and also for peaceful life upon earth.

I would also tell him to learn and to think for himself the ways he would serve the Lord. In this thought and in this undertaking of his he will inevitably find the way of serving his fellow men. For his faith would then be manifested by His conduct. If Christians behave in this way, if we dedicate ourselves to this fundamental task, then we will have a peaceful world and will be assured of not transgressing against the will and the Commandments of God.

Dr. Hoffman: Your Imperial Majesty, are there any incidents in your life which stand in your memory as times when faith in Christ sustained you?

H.I.M. Haile Selassie I: There are many instances in my life where the belief in The Almighty and the Christian Faith have sustained me, times of troubles and difficulties. No matter what may befall a human being he can always succeed in overcoming it in time if he has the strength of faith and praise to God, for inevitably He comes to the assistance of those that believe in HIM and those that through their work live an exemplary life.

This goes not only for Christians in my view, but for all men. I think God communicates with those that find themselves in misfortune. In particular, when my country Ethiopia was invaded by aliens several years ago I was sustained in that period by my faith in God and in the abiding belief that justice, however it may take time, will ultimately prevail.

If I did not have faith in The Almighty and in His Righteousness and that justice inevitable prevails, then I would have lost hope and thus the interests of my country would have been ignored. Because I attempted to maintain my faith in HIM and because all Ethiopians maintained their faith in the ultimate goodness of the world and in the grand design that The Almighty has for all men in the world, we were able to victoriously re-enter our country and rid ourselves of evil forces.

If I did not have in my heart the love of God I don't think I would have acted in a manner that I did. The love of God brings a sense of religiousness in a human being, it gives him comfort for the future and assurance that right cause will ultimately prevail.

DR. HOFFMAN: His Imperial Majesty Emperor Haile Selassie The First ascended the throne of Ethiopia in November in the year 1930. Now, in the year 1968, Haile Selassie has been in the forefront in mediating the crisis in Biafra. Some of the intervening years have been stormy ones. But there are few Statesmen who can retrace a career of more resolute leadership in both internal and world affairs. Few can claim greater unbroken continuity with the past that nevertheless moves methodically into the twentieth century. At the same time, few have seen more anguish and defeat than Haile Selassie, of whom biographer Leonard Mosley has written in projected epitaph, He shaped, rather than waited upon events.

Just seven months after He became Emperor in 1930, He gave the people of Ethiopia their first written Constitution. His plea before the League of Nations in 1936 as His country was ravaged by Mussolini's armies, and His anguished exile during the following years, are etched in the memory of the world. When He regained His throne in 1941, His refusal to allow retaliation against the defeated invader was viewed with disbelief.

"On this day," He said, " I owe thanks unutterable by the mouth of man to the living God who has enabled me to be present among you. Today is the beginning of a new era in the history of Ethiopia. Since this is so, do not reward evil for evil.. do not commit any act of cruelty like those which the enemy committed against us up to this present time.

DR. HOFFMANN: When the United Nations Charter was drawn up after World War II His Imperial Majesty Haile Selassie was one of its original drafters. In 1963, He established the Organization of African Unity, to encourage co-operation among African States and co-ordinate their efforts to build a better life for the people of all Africa.

Constitutional reforms in 1956 guaranteed all the rights of the people of Ethiopia, though the Emperor retains much personal power in governing His agricultural nation of 22 million people, all the time seeking to lead His nation toward a fully modern way of life.

At 76 years of age, His Imperial Majesty continues to work a twenty hour day, with three hours for sleep and one devoted to prayer. Emperor Haile Selassie and I talked about many things on that day during the rainy season.

DR. HOFFMAN: Your Imperial Majesty, how does it seem to you the Apostle Paul meant by the statement, Faith works by love?

H.I.M. Haile Selassie I: What St. Paul said here is not a mistaken statement. You all know what St. Paul was and what kind of work he was engaged in before his conversion. Later on, after his conversion he had faith and love, and if he had not had that he would not have taught people this in his epistles. Neither love nor faith are separable from each other.

An elaboration of this is Paul's exposition in one of his Epistles which speak of love and faith. Without love all of our human efforts in the sight of God can be useless. He loved us and on our behalf He was given as a ransom, and it was because of love and His love for us that He accomplished the act of love.

Dr. Hoffman: Your Imperial Majesty, as a member of the Body of Christ, what do you expect of the Church?

H.I.M. Haile Selassie I: The Church is not merely a building. The Church is the faithful fulfilment of the Christian life and its requirements. Thus, as the name applies to the buildings so is our heart The Church in which God dwells.

After our blameless Creator was sent to this world by His Father, then the hearts of all believers become The Temple of God. The love of God cannot be fathomed by a series of questions and answers, and man's soul cannot experience deeper enrichment as a result. We believe that men at all times be bound by His love and grace.

DR. HOFFMAN: Your Imperial Majesty, as a member of the body of Christ, what do you feel you can contribute to The Church?

H.I.M. HAILE SELASSIE I: All men are endowed with natural responsibility. This responsibility is in turn distributed and delegated to all according to his gift, and it is expected of each one to fulfil his responsibility. This responsibility in turn is to God and thus for example, and would start his work asking God to bless the beginning and thank God for a good ending too.

We believe that all people in all of their responsibilities delegated to them will begin and finish their work in God's name. I gave you brief answer. If we go into detail we would have to spend a long time discussing.

DR. HOFFMAN: It is a magnificent answer and I am deeply grateful for it. To turn to another subject, Your Imperial Majesty, are there any passages of the bible that have become especially meaningful to you?

H.I.M. HAILE SELASSIE I: I have the highest respect for the Bible as a whole. We also recognise the rightful name the Bible bears. We find that in all the periods of the Old Testament, in the time of Patriarchs, Kings, and Prophets, great miracles were done. On the other hand, the time in which Our Lord HIM-self gave the command to go to all the world and to preach is also of high value. Then, Matthew, Mark, Luke and John,- the four gospels in which the sayings of our Lord are recorded- are pillars for all men on the earth. Therefore the Bible should not be cut into portions.

DR. HOFFMAN: As a mature Christian, have You a special word for young people of these days?

H.I.M. HAILE SELASSIE I: On this occasion I address all those within Our Empire. Our Christianity is not restricted to a given church and I stress above all that We do not wish to make distinctions. My advice to all is to fulfil the Ten Commandments. You are aware of the contents of the Ten Commandments and can elaborate on it. If the nation for which I am the Emperor follows and accepts this, since its also what I accept and follow, I would believe our country is not only historically Christian but also actively Christian.

DR. HOFFMAN: Your Imperial Majesty, the birthday of Our Lord is observed by peoples throughout the world in different ways, I know, and I should like to ask You how You observe the feast of the nativity of our Lord within Your own family and household?

H.I.M. HAILE SELASSIE I: The birth of Our Lord is a joyous family event. However, I do not only rejoice with my kindred and family since the whole Ethiopian nation is my family. I say this in the context of Christmas being observed by all churches in Ethiopia. I rejoice on this occasion also because of Jesus Christ being given for us. For He was born in the lowly place and got warmth by animals. This fact encourages us to celebrate it with joy.

When I have visited the five large continents, I have not been anywhere where there was not a church. All over the world I have come to know that the birth of Jesus Christ is celebrated.

DR. HOFFMAN: Your Imperial Majesty, as a figure of world importance and probably one of the best known man in the world today, I should like to ask You this question: What meaning can the birth of Christ have for the nations of the world today?

H.I.M. HAILE SELASSIE I: As I said before, the birth of Christ is celebrated all over the world. When I say the whole world it does not mean that all people would observe it in the same manner. In all the places that I have visited, including the Muslims and the Buddhists, We have seen the observance. But for Christians it is an act conducted with love.

DR. HOFFMAN: Your Imperial Majesty, You have done us great honour and also all the people who will listen to this broadcast by giving us the opportunity to speak with You this day. And all those who are listening should know that this conversation was held in the Imperial Palace at Addis Ababa, Ethiopia, with His Imperial Majesty the Emperor of Ethiopia, Haile Selassie I, and we thank You and wish you God's blessing in all the days to come.

H.I.M. HAILE SELASSIE I: Thank you.

አባ ቅዱስ

St. John Chapter 17, Verse 11

"And now I am no more in the world, but these are in the world, and I come to thee. **ቅዱስ አባት ሆይ፥** [Oh] Holy Father, keep through thine own name those whom thou hast given me, that they may be one, as we are."

Printed in Great Britain
by Amazon